THE
DOPPELGANGER
DID IT!

Where The Past is Now Present!

DAVID MILES

Table of Contents

Authors Biography iv
Acknowledgement v
Preface vi
Dedication x
Introduction. xv
Review... by Shelby Alcott. & Sandy Schultz xii
Book Club Members. xiii

Chapter One   The Past Came Back...Again 19

Chapter Two   What's an "In (en) cumbent," to do? 34

Chapter Three   Before "It" comes back, At Us Again 55

Chapter Four   The Land of Confusion?. 73

Chapter Five   Can You DIG IT? 89

Chapter Six   *Pain* has NO home...
                 It goes anywhere "it" wants 99

Chapter Seven   You *will* Really Get A "Charge"
                 out of This!. 119

Chapter Eight   "The Past IS – *Present!*...again" 150

Chapter Nine   The END IS NEAR! 155

Authors Biography

Associates Degree	Concordia College, Milwaukee, WI.
Bachelor of Arts Degree	Concordia University River Forest, Ill.
Certified Financial Counselor	Crown Financial Ministries, Ga.
Ordained Pastoral Ministries	Fellowship Bible Ministries, Milwaukee, WI.
Vice President	Oak Creek MotorSports
Certified small engine mechanic	Evinrude Motor, Arctic Cat Co. Briggs&StrattonCo. Kawasaki Motor Corp USA
Corp. Store Manager: Batteries Plus	Certified Battery Technician: Batteries Plus LLC.

Regional Sales Manager: Interstate Batteries

Corp. Store Manager: Schlossmann Triumph City

Corp. Store Sales Mgr.: Advance R.V. & Camping

Acknowledgements

All of the incredible people who came to my rescue, on the usually busy intersection, just south of Milwaukee Wisconsin. And to the hospital personnel that did such a Great job on keeping me alive (again).

To my dear wife, who {repeatedly} ends up at St. Lou's Hospital in the emergency room awaiting the outcome of my dramatic impact(s).

To all of the people who helped me edit this book

Most of ALL! The God of Heaven, who…while allowing me to go through all of these astonishing events; has "NEVER let me go." Seriously… now looking back through all of these pages, and musing over my own unwritten memories, I can clearly see His hand swaddling each and every part of my existence.

Hopefully, you'll see as you read on; that my personal belief in my Savior, Jesus Christ, made all the difference to my eternal life. Were it not for His perfect life and sacrificial death, this whole book would be a mute-point in history, as well as my presence on this earth.

Preface

Those of you who have read my first book "<u>The DOA Who Made It</u>" certainly will see, and most assuredly agree that this just has to be some sort of total enigma, that is "supernatural" or a kind of "Deja vu", to happen again and again, so precise, and exact. All of the various dictionaries and even "Wikipedia;" all label those sort of instances or occurrences as a "phenomenon."

"Doppelganger" is the only word that I could find to answer such a condition. That German word that we nonchalantly slid into our vocabulary simply means {ghost-shadow-duplicate-or replica}. After reading this story; please make me aware.

I deeply and seriously love my wife and two boys; as I have for now over twenty years. I love to go to church; for two distinct reasons 1. Learn and worship 2. To find who or what I can help in my little circle of life here in Southeast Wisconsin. I'm a firm believer, in the concept of trying as hard as I can, to do well to others. My faith in God has burned in me to follow the principles of doing right to others. Which is why I find it so "goofy-corny-and far less than accurate," that anyone can be an evolutionist or Atheist. Whose base reasoning is "the strong survive."

So, with that premise, that "only the strong survive" where does empathy, sympathy, giving and "blessing" others appear from? Do you see my point? Only after I came to have a true spiritual relationship with God and my savior Jesus Christ; did I get the concern for others well-being, as well as my own.

So, while telling a person this story, one day, he listened intently with great interest, and when I had finished, he looked at me and said "Ipse-dixit," which translated direct from Latin to mean "that's just how it is". "What?" I gulped. "Aren't you also going to say something like that's just your fate I guess?" He then nodded in agreement with his own description, as he turned and walked away.

That would be a "pardonable" quip of an answer, but just keep reading this book, and you'll say to yourself, the word "phenomenon" simply does not do justice to define what happened to David, in such a remarkably duplicated format. Especially when you are dealing with five different individual human beings. Which is why I am not as willing to accept that as a definition either; although being as close to accurate, but too vague. And it still doesn't note the replicating of itself on such a large scale, and so precisely identical. To the same individual, at the same time, in the same place, going in the same direction, as well as some of the exact same people; six years later. Which seems to me that the only real name and designation can be that the….

"The DOPPELGANGER DID IT!".

I do, genuinely hope that you will have come to a hopefully clear and agreeable understanding, as well, and then full acceptance, that there is absolutely NO possible way to label any of this as some sort of COINCIDENCE!

While being in the "unbelievable span of six years, how could anyone, anywhere, or in any way, arrange or orchestrate such a thing? So... if YOU just can't get yourself to accept what I classified as "Providence" then don't make yourself go any further.

But...if you do accept the definition of "Providence-Deity influence" then you will just love what you read here.

There are a few intense and exciting section, along with a smattering of silly/ funny ones as well. Unimaginable occurrence's, that one individual from the upper-Midwest, would never be able to imagine this happening to him, but actually kept "piling" onto his life. Go Figure... I am sure that you will enjoy the read.

Just to give you a taste of the first book that I wrote, known as The DOA Who Made It! Here are a few paragraphs to captivate your interest.

The D.O.A.....Who Made
This is the true story of
David Miles, actual life & Death experience

Its' Not just another action packed type exciting book about someone who's seen a light at the end of a tunnel (usually a train coming).
It is a very stirring, stimulating, introspection, as to the reality of LIFE! Here and Here-After.

Coming back to life, I gained the title: "<u>The D.O. A. who Made It</u>" Ya... I made it back to this life; this time, but what about the next?

So what happens after YOU die? Do You really Know? Science reports what they think they know. I WILL tell you what I Do Know For Sure!

Life doesn't end at death. Eternity awaits. You ARE going somewhere, when YOU Die!

Do you want to know your destination? Just get a hold of a G.P.S. For life (the Bible)

It is so hard to understand something you have never experienced, until you listen to someone who has been there or gone through it.

Motorcycles figure heavily in my life. This book will entertain you immensely; even if You either "Love 'em or Hate 'em. Without guns or bullets, there is still enough action in this read.

These words describe (yes again) my personal journey from LIFE to DEATH & back to LIFE, again; and they will illuminate your path should you choose to travel down it.

Dedication

To all of my faithful readers of "The DOA Who Made It" – thank you, so much. And as well as all of you folks who listened to my many presentations and still bought and read the book. – Thank You

And just think of all those students who had me as their "Substitute Teacher" and lived to talk about it, ha ha. They would clearly tell me repeatedly how much they enjoyed the stories. [In today's age, the school kids, would just pull out their smart phones and look "it up" on line, and verify my claim to being an author. They were all impressed that the book is getting 4 & 5 stars, for all of those who reviewed it received on-line. And for all the middle, and high school students that bought the book, and when I came back to their school, they couldn't wait to tell me that they just loved the book, which I was then required to autograph it, for them; just in case it does become a motion picture. They can let everyone in their life know that they knew me way before it becomes a movie. What an endorsement. Thanks, Kids!

Then there is aa fellow named Dayton Davenport who was there to support me all of the way through, both books, and his friendship and assistance puts me deeply in gratitude in his debt.

My special appreciation goes to my Heavenly Father, and Savior, for proving Himself to me, even once again; and of course, allowing me to live to tell all of these horrendous experiences. I have NO idea as to why these things have all happening, especially to me, but as long as He gets the glory. That is all that matters.

Review's By

The {most honorable *Elder*} Mr. Shelby Alcott
Layton Avenue Baptist Church:
"These two books about Dave's life and death are....
so compelling and spiritually interesting."

Mrs. Sandy Schultz RN:
"Both stories are just so fascinating and together
they are so unbelievable; yet true."

RPH. Jessica Battaglia:
"Very impactful"

The Distinguished" Dayton Davenport:
"Spiritually provoking"

Book Club Members

Here is a gift just for all of you!

A fter you have purchased "The Doppelganger Did It" and started enjoying the read.

You will have become qualified to contact me via Facebook, or the e-mail site.

"The DOA Who Made It!

Any time after you get started; You can send me your request for the number of copies that you would like and just include one of the UPC code numbers (that is the numbers on the bottom of the bar code).

We will then be able to send you and your club members (1 copy each) of the first book "The DOA Who Made It!" for only $9.95 for each copy you would like.

That's almost half price for each!!

Your club will then be able to engage in the whole story from beginning till now. There are so many more fascinating events that have taken place; You won't want to miss.

And, Better YET!

I will personally autograph each and every copy and if you give me the correct information I will be glad to address it to whomever you would like.

I will also include the month and date; since so many folks are waiting for it to become a motion picture, someday. (Both books together- most likely)

Please make sure that you give me the correct mailing address for the book.

The minimal cost of shipping will be only $1.00 per auto-graphed book.

If preferred you can call or email me for the mailing address or just call

1-414-281-9118 with you card #, (so it doesn't go out on the internet).

Enjoy the WHOLE Remarkable story.

And, please share the exciting information with others, so they too can be inspired.

Introduction

1. So…How could this even be?
2. NO, rather: How, could {this} be real, not imagined?
3. This just can't be happening; right not like this?
4. It conclusively, has to be totally impossible!
5. Maybe a horrific "nightmare;" gone wrong?
6. A warp, in the "space-time" continuum?

So which answer is true?

O ……………None of the above!

O ……………Some of the above!

O ……………All of the above! {Hint} the first 2 aren't right

NO-ONE, could believe that something like this could be true, but all of it is!

Two completely separate police departments and almost innumerable pages in the

Very large and busy trauma hospital where he almost spent his last hours on earth and twice at that.

Just read on, and conclude for yourself, how come it is required to see how this whole story comes together; in nothing short of miraculous ways.

As he rapidly swung his not so long right leg up and over the saddle of his sport touring Concours motorcycle; which was the same one he had been driving now for the last six years. Dave was visibly excited as most cyclists are in spring juts waiting to take his first motorcycle ride of the New Year. Even though he was about to leave work, at his retail power-sports store, the experienced motorcycle driver took full account that it was unusually warm, and cloud free, here on that mid-March late afternoon at 6:00 pm. Unlike his first "mishap" on a hot sunny Jul 1st, today was one which was still before the "Daylight Savings Time change." The roads were dry and clean, and indisputably like almost every cyclists, Dave couldn't wait to go for his first ride of the new season. He rapidly got his cycle running {of course; it was a Kawasaki} and he then proceeded to take-off from the parking lot, heading north like always towards home, which was straight up the road. He got onto the big main highway that was right out in front of the long glass fronted showroom building. Again, as in all six work-days a week, he was headed out and was just going back to home

Only, this time, just like nearly six years prior, it would {once again} Not be a so called "normal or casual ride" home. He was set to thoroughly enjoy every minute of that sweet ride. (Yup… here we go again-"Oh NO)!" It wasn't quite a mile up to the next, often time's frenzied and large hectic intersection. It is designed with lane turning lights and two lanes going straight and a third for right turns. Dave is, as usual, approaching the cross road, this time in the right lane, when he saw a white car pull up from the east, headed straight west toward another suburb of Milwaukee, Wisconsin. As the car slowed down to stop at it's now red light; all seemed well, and relatively quiet, going both directions and even the cross road. The street light turned green for Dave about 2 or 3 blocks from intersecting as he was approaching it.

He continued going straight in the right lane, doing about 40 miles an hour. Just as he entered the intersection and passed in front of the white car {waiting for his greenlight}, he instantly recognized a driver's car mirror, less than two feet in front of him.

He knew that this was really going to Hurt; if not KILL him AGAIN! What Again? What's that all about?

"Oh NO!" he screamed to himself. [I'm gonna "get IT "right here again!] But THIS just Can't be! It is just to bizarre to even so much as imagine

Bu sure enough... "Here we go again." It IS taking place exactly like before; "all over"

Could this have been Dave's "Doppelganger"? Or WHAT? Could this same thing be possibly happen again; with "everything "just exactly the same, right here, & right Now, too? There's NO WAY "All of this" could coincide ...exactly the same- it's just too impossible even to imagine, especially like this, to ME...!

But, YES, IT DID take place just exactly like the "first one". Only a few slight variations but sooo... many "duplications". Dave's first story was bizarre, but this is downright unimaginably "freaky".

Please God?... "What are You trying to tell me"

What*ever* you do; don't ask "What did I do wrong?" Or "why are you punishing me like this?" If you have never made a personal acceptance of Jesus becoming your "sole" source for your eternal destiny, then you could ask why am I being punished. Or having all of these circumstance befall you. But you don't know "Gods punishment" yet.

However, If you have, at some point in your life, humbled yourself enough to cry out to God to save you, with the trust that His blood washed away all of your sins; you won't be "punished" again or some more by God, for He has already taken that type of punishment away.

The true definition of punishment is "to inflict a penalty or subject to pain loss or confinement. You will NOT be punished again for your imperfections (sins). But You will be chastened. That simply means (corrected) to make you better; (in God's eyes).

What *Is* taking place is (as you will read in this book) God is doing a "unique" service to you to become more of what you should be. Remember, He makes NO mistakes, all of these occurrences, are nothing but for you good and His glory. It sure doesn't seem or feel that way while going through it, but in time it always does show true.

Chapter One

"The Past Came Back!...Again"

Lying in the median, flat on my back, in an almost mind numbing and dizzying type of stupor. It was clear that the tentacles of that morbid beast we call *death* was going to wrap its grip around me yet once more. It really looked like it would be *this* time for sure. But, being *unable* to breathe, leaves little doubt that the "inevitable" is here.

Cavorting through the air, and rapidly dropping to the hard pavement, and hood of a car as well, made me resolute in my deep seated suspicions of the annihilation that I was quickly, about to experience. The human body can "just take so much;" and with this being my third encounter with facing the grim reaper. I'd rather resigned myself to hat I thought was reality' this time... "My Life Is OVER!"

I had absolutely NO sense of feeling... arms, trunk legs, fingers, *lips, tongue NOTHING!* But then again, I couldn't feel myself breathing either....because I wasn't breathing. 'Here I come," was all that I could think.

Granted; I certainly did NOT have much joy for this large {well lit} intersection, anyway. As you may already know, or will shortly find out quickly. It did leave a lot to be desired, in my memories. Since my sudden literal "death experience" right there had given me reverberating horror; just a few short six years earlier. Yes it did sour my feelings of driving, especially while being right at "my fateful" cross-way. But non-the-less it was about my only route home from where I was employed for the last twenty seven years. I lived four miles straight north of work, and this was just one mile from there.

But not really giving any particular thought of my earlier termination incident, I was just passing through; again, like always, for I had, nevertheless taken it, hundreds, no thousands of times before, in the last 20 some years.

Yes, I will admit that my "cautious apprehension" for this normally busy intersection, had started to somewhat wane. Now, never imagining that 6 years ago, might have just been a rehearsal for this afternoon? Maybe a harbinger? Or Precursor? Was there anybody who offered me a presage warning of a dualistic event? Oh, I got lots of "cautionary reprimands." It seems when there is a traumatic occurrence that takes place; all of the "fifth quarter couch potatoes" come out to give their admonishments.

Before I expound on the whole second chapter of "27th & Rawson" in my life and near death…again. I would prepare you for just what came after. See this time I didn't die or enter a comma. Maybe this section of my story will give you greater appreciation of the severity of my second "happening."

Could "Fate" be "Late"?

So, here is the "sneak peak" of my <u>conscious</u> visit into the hospital. (Due to this very exasperating event that is) As the story proceeds you will see why it was such a "big event" in my life (clearly once again). I don't have any idea what is the point behind all of this occurring, to me. Excepting to say that "somehow" I do believe that there is PROVIDENTIAL conditions taking place here. Which is where I believe the real answer truly lies. What else could it be? Should we just say "it is All a Big Coincidence?" Or maybe the "Ultimate "Just So Happens?" When you get done reading this absolutely true story; you too will have to become a believer in something. Be it the two different police reports on file, or the hospital records and numerous witness and staff testimonies, this just can't or couldn't be arranged or "concocted." I'll be saying this over and over not to be repetitive and boring, but rather to drive home the impact and significance of all of the explicit duplications (that just couldn't be man-made) that took place from six years prior.

Laying there in that very same rather open and quite busy seemingly almost chaotic, emergency room, just like I had six years ago, yet this time was much different, since I was fully conscious, and awake and able to take everything in. Yet still in a "mummified" like condition, hardly able to make any movements. (Can we say shock, anyone?) All of this, after now my third "death defying" misadventure, I was not so much in pain; because I was quite accurately still in a state of bewilderment, but just trying to fathom how and why all of this could be playing out so precisely the same as when I had become rather "well known" as <u>**The DOA Who Made It?**</u> **Right there in that very same hospital's emergency room, the very same time of day, even once again. I laid there in agonizing pain (now it was starting to hit me more and more,) ruminating on just how this new occurrence can even be true?**

Someone! "Please tell me! What did I do to deserve all this? Three horrifically painful and agonizing (death defying) crashes?" Ok' I know that you will say "see how dangerous motorcycles are?" "Ye but what about a six-wheeler ATV, In a parking lot? Really- that too?" If you read any of my first book, and plan to get "into" this one; you'll know motorcycles actually had nothing to do with any of these incidents.

I will say this for the hospital staff, that shortly after they put me in a little cul-de-sac of an opening that would hold a bed and some workers'. It almost made me feel like it felt more like a stanchion. No walls, just curtains, and absolutely No tranquility with hoses and wire attached to my body, like a cow getting ready to be milked. No such thing as any privacy, there either; (those poor Kaw's-oops I meant dairy cows) when they finally got me completely "hooked up" to oxygen and the saline bag.

Surprising me yet even more, was the arrival of a young man from our church, who was a big help in our AWANA program, and was very involved in the Friday night Bible studies that we held at our house, for now the last twelve years. He suddenly showed up at the foot of my bed, before anyone else that I knew, and came and sat with me. He was trying to lighten my ubiquitous agony, by being very silly. {It helped a little} He was always good at making me laugh. That Tom is some character. I questioned him. "How did you even know that I was here?" I was at

AWANA when your wife called and told me that you wouldn't be at AWANA tonight." "So I hurried up, and shot down here, figuring almost for sure that this is where they would bring you." "So Elsbeth knows already too?" "Yup, she's on her way here too." He came back with.

Every Wednesday evening, our church held a really super neat "kids program" that is called "A.W.A.N.A."; which stands proudly for "Approved Workmen Are Not Ashamed." It is part of a Bible quote from the New Testament book of II Timothy 2:15, and it is such a great children's program that our church would pick up "loads" of third through twelfth graders many others were dropped off, and we like thousands of churches, world-wide; it would give them an hour & a half of fun and caring and clear simple moral values. Not only that, but a lot of the poor and inner-city children and even kids from around our church's neighborhoods or the suburbs, seldom were able to "revere" that space in time, like these boys and girls who got a little reprieve from their typical domesticated lifestyles would allow.

I Don't "AWANA" go home.

The founder of that organization, which began in 1950 was a pastor from a large Christian church in downtown Chicago, called The Northside Gospel Center. As I shared in my last book, the woman who with her husband, had been missionaries with another organization called New Tribes Bible Institute, which was yet another entity he help get founded. This man, Dr. Lance Latham and his wonderful wife "Teach," ministered to so many people for so many years, that you just can't believe how much of their own lives, they GAVE to help others!

I was privileged to become a good friend of his, and would be willing to sit for hours listening and learning from him. He had so much knowledge and not only of the Bible, but life values in general. He had so much of the Bible memorized word for word perfectly that, even in his eighties he could remember most all of them and teach from them clearly .

When he would give a Bible study up at the youth camp in east central Wisconsin, aptly named Camp AWANA, surprise! He would open his Bible and read some verses before he would expound on them. The only secret to all of us listeners, was that he would be reading, say Romans chapter six but he bible was open to maybe the Gospel of John or Mark.

"What NO Blood?

Ok, Ok, Sorry, I digressed. Now back to the hospital emergency room and my lovely accommodations. All sorts of medical staff, kept coming and going in and out checking my chest, and my blood pressure and heart rate. This time there wasn't any blood loss to speak of but they sure knew that the whole right side of my chest was collapsed down flat, into a cavity where my right lung and ribs should be residing. One of the nurses slid her hands up and down around both of my legs, feeling for injuries, I suppose; but that really felt weird.

When I finally could recognize the young man Tom, as he was being so jovial; I queried him; "did you take off my pants and under pants? A quick clear "Nope-not me. Dave." My facial expression must have been clue enough of my repugnancy of that predicament. They had my neck in some kind of a prosthetic like stay, which prevented me from bending my head forward, to look down. I couldn't really make much of any sounds but a few faint gruff's, and even that was excruciatingly painful.

My wife arrived, after I had been lying there for about a half hour. She clearly knew her way around, since, not a lot of changes had been made to that emergency room in the last six years. It was one location that I had wished she never would have had to meet me; especially having now had to almost temporarily reside there again. She had spent an agonizing six hours at my first big injury. And here we are again. "Sorry honey." I will say one thing though, I was really glad that none of the medical staff said "Hi Elsbeth; how are You doing this year?"

But, I had just wished they would have given me some pain medicine, other than a couple of Tylenols. Those "pain killers" were definitely over powered by my body's trumpeting cry of living horror. What sincerely seemed to hurt the most, {if I could honestly segment it,} was the front area of my upper right hand side of my chest. Unbeknown to me at the time, what I was shortly to be made aware of, on my little excursion, up to the ICU ward, was that all of my ribs, on the right hand side of my body, were crushed in and they were sure that my right lung was no longer functioning. That certainly didn't sound good to me even in my heightened state of delirium. How would they know all of that? Apparently down in the emergency, when I had first arrived they took some type of rolling ex-ray machine and made their determinations upon that news, which later they informed me

25

why it took so long, down in the emergency room, again. Alright already; so we know I am obviously no medical whiz.

I had no idea why Elsbeth (my wife) didn't accompany me up there. But I will say, that to this day, I sure am thankful that she did not escort me up to, that "locker of humility that I was about to experience. Though, on the way up, I mused to myself, how this "accident" was so much more painful than the last. But let's be honest, the last big one, those six years ago, I was in a coma. So I didn't feel pain {I guess} so they say. Does that mean that it doesn't count? Hmmm

It's best if *I* HAND IT TO YA!

Finally, after those many long hours of enormous pain, and their poking all around my torso. It was deemed that I should eventually be transferred up to ICU, in that big traumatic hospital. Then about another three to four hours of intense agony, in that emergency room, they did finally get me up into the Intensive Care Unit. Everything moved pretty fast; till then. As I have just shared, going up in the elevator on the gurney with my skating saline carrier and bag alongside. I suppose that it was an "orderly" who pushed me, when we went in and up, then we got off of that elevator. I felt like I was almost launched, into very a large brightly lit open room, it was where they could have cordoned off smaller sections with just a high sliding curtain, but there were none closed when I arrived.

Some form of medical female (I think). Came over and pulled the head of my bed, up towards the one far back wall. At that vantage point I could see the rest of the whole room, once they adjusted my bed to tilt up. They obviously could all see me as well; because my head was slightly canted up, to compensate for the oxygen machine and the guard over my nose and mouth as well as various hoses. There were a lot of women dressed in medical attire. "Zooming" around in that room, which seemed almost like they were honey bees, just "dashing" around in and out of the (hive) room. But nobody seemed to have anything to do with me, other than just let me lay there. So now what is going to be done up here? I questioningly queried to myself, because I really had no idea, what might be next.

I am about to embark on a description here, of something so personally mind boggling to me as an individual that it became "burned" into my consciousness like nothing else. It literally removed the pain for a three to five minute period of my life, and brought me to my knees emotionally. Please don't take this wrong, but just watch how during this medical experience of fear, horror, and trauma, there can even be moments of psychological drama that are equally as powerful.

"Going for a Stroll"

Sometime later, (maybe half an hour or so) a smaller petite size brunette nurse {I believe}; started walking towards me. She looked to be about only in her early to mid-twenties, I noticed that she was wearing {what I would say was} a rather "tight-fitting" nurse's uniform which rode up very high towards her waist. I saw her making her approach toward the foot of my bed, then abruptly stopped immediately behind its frame. Without so much as saying a word or making any sounds or even looking me in the face. She stepped right up to the end of the bed and took the little stool which she had in her hand and set it down right at the back of my elaborate medical trundle.

Aligning it up to just the right of the center of the bed frame, I happened to notice that she set something in a plastic wrap on the top of the mattress as well, which at that time, I couldn't discern, as to what it was. After removing her slip-off type white loafers, she stepped up on the stool and slid her one knee up forward towards me across the back of the mattress closer to my body.

Quickly, after raising that snugly fit uniform, yet again, once more to improve her leg movement, she came a little closer to me and then pulled her other leg up on the other side of my legs, and then she proceeded to crawl slowly up towards my mid trunk area and shockingly close to my head and oxygen mask which was of course still in place over my nose and mouth, leaving my range of vision quite wide and clear. And far better than any full face helmet ever could. But she did move my head and upper body bed parts back to horizontal, so I couldn't look forward anymore just vertical.

Here is where she then stood straight up and straddled her torso on either side of mine, she was now facing the back wall. Then she began stepping towards my head, even closer. Now this was beginning to get real awkward and more psychologically painful. If that could even be possible.

Actually, even though I had that oxygen mask on, as so I was able to continue breathing; I could see her bare-skin legs and that almost "miniskirt-ish" white uniform fit and extremely snug uniform, come right up and over my head and mask. That's where I was able to do little more than be allowed to look straight up, and that was it. I Will Not tell you if she had any panties on. But

I will state that she was not wearing any kind of hosiery, either stockings or panty hose. So now, you see why I was so thankful my wife was NOT there to observe all of that. But, as a matter of fact, looking back at this (one-time hopefully) event, maybe it was all done as part of her strategy. (?)

At this juncture, she was standing directly over my face. And of course the devices that I had on. The only other option that I had, was to squeeze my eyes shut; but that even hurt...really it did. Other than that, all I was allowed to do, was little more than look straight up, under her skirt. Fully aware of what was taking place, it was also quite apparent that this nurse was rather "unabashed" at her achievements. Interesting enough, I wasn't chilled anymore just then either.

Then to switch sides with her feet and legs, she proceeded to do a quick little "twisty jump" right on the mattes and she even bounced a little she turn her whole body to now be aiming in the same direction as I was facing. She simply lowered herself down again to her knees to a crawl sort of position, just above my chest. It seemed as if she was now likely going to work her way towards my lower trunk. But then, while sliding her miniskirt bottom even higher towards her waist, to giver her complete freedom of movement for her body and her legs. Once again on her knees, she then landed each limb over and around my waist, while still leaning far forward. This is so weird, I had no idea about what was to come.

That now being tensely bizarre enough for me to observe, she pointedly bowed forward even more towards the foot of my bunk and grabbed the covers that were shielding my feet and legs, which they had placed over my lower body, to cover me down in the emergency room knowing that I would be feeling very chilled. At that, in a graceful sort of way, she pulled the sheet and the comforter up and over my legs to gather them to the middle of my waist, andtoward herself. I am sure you can now imagine just what's going through my head, as I could faintly realize that she then grabbed ahold of my hospital gown also, (which closes in the back) and raised that upwards towards my trunk, as well. I'm beginning to almost panic, wondering "just what's going on here?" "Oh please, NO!" I thought to myself.

Rabidly, bending forward further, after she exposed my "whole life" to the world; she grabbed all of my "manhood" and clinched it like a broom handle, (nothing dainty) and continued her agenda. She then bent over even farther, her face now very close to my "personal life," and I saw her reach over to the lower part of the bed again and grab that item that I couldn't previously identify.

Swiftly surmising my fate. She ripped the package open, and while holding on rather "tight" to {yes me,} continued her progress, which I abruptly found out, was to insert a very stiff, cold, large long "soda-straw like hard plastic tube down the inside of my shank. OOOhhh—-!

I "forthwith" jerked and squirmed while I quietly screamed to myself, as she advanced her modus operandi of putting a "catheter" into me. I humbly and squeakily questioned her by inquiring; "doesn't this bother you? Because as you now well know, it sure is "bothering" me!" As I am confident she had become very well aware of by her own doing, at that moment. Both I and the catheter were standing at attention and I honestly

30

had "NO control" over any of this situation that was going on to my body.

When I repeated the question to her, all she replied, now while she was almost sitting on my waist, with her back still toward me, was "hey ya seen one – ya seen 'em all". You could almost see the big "smirky" grin on her face, with that quip. But those words surely didn't give me much comfort or resolution, now that I am in a state and condition of being so abashedly her hostage. Even as she "flung" my gown and the covers back to my lower extremities; she proceeded to quite carefully, crawl back down to the foot of the bed, turn around a second time, and step off the bed to put her shoes back on and grab the stool, and simply stroll away.

That interaction finally being over, I regained the feeling of ALL of my existing pain. Helping relieve me of the chills, and warm up; I knew that I NEVER wanted to experience or repeat anything like that ever again; and I mean; for as long as I live. Whew!

Having never before, been so blatantly humiliated, all I thought was "be merciful to me Oh Lord;" so I never have to go through anything like that ever again in my lifetime, here on earth. Then I did qualify it by praying "At least while I'm conscious."

A short time later, my wife came up to my side, at which point I quite obviously did not utter a word about that "short little" affair.

After she left for the night to get home to be with our boys, now ten and fifteen years old. I laid there getting almost no sleep due to the extremity of the pain; I began to ruminate my actions and experiences of that afternoons adventures which I had once more been partaker of.

A *salient* solution

There is not a soul one earth, that could call what I am about to divulge as being pure duplication, or simply a form of "similarity." So then, just what is going on here?" How could anyone or anything arrange or compose, or actually organize such a replication of thing six years into the future? Could the president? The Pope? Or who? No one I know could possibly orchestrate something like that. Be there five different individuals with absolutely NO Other contacts, have something like this be so precisely identical in location, time, and all other conditions. There is no algorithm or program that could align and arrange all of this now almost six years later.)

Later that evening, they finally gave me some pain medicine, so I could sleep, but it didn't really help all that much. Not looking for any sympathy, I can say that I have grown accustom to a lot of pain in my body. The ramifications from my first 27th St. incident still linger and abided with me daily, with pangs of discomfort.

It is hard to imagine getting "used to pain" but just ask anyone who is inflicted with such, and you will hear complete agreement, with that statement. All any of us can say is "You've– just gotta live with it!" I mentioned casually (in my first book), that I had an encounter with {what I'll say right now} the "BIG MAN" upstairs. He came down to visit me in my room, on the 8th floor of the hospital. We had quite the conversation, that evening (July 15th 1986). The medical issues that I had talked to him about in that room, were only the ones that I was aware of at the time. Apologetically he expressed His sorrow for that pain that I was suffering, but promised to take it away. And He DID! I have regained the strength and ability that someone of my present age, should have. How neat is that; HUH?

Yes, I am still afflicted with some degree of (reciprocating) issues. I just have to say that like the man known as the Apostle Paul in the New Testament of the Bible; when he prayed for relief from his painful issues, all God said to him was "My Grace is Sufficient for Thee." So I have nothing to really complain about; especially while talking to other people in my generation, it might just be age that is "showing its face, now.

While expressing the fact that there truly is so much pain and suffering on this earth. His abode (heaven) is SOOoo much Greater; with NO pain or suffering. He is so sorry that we all don't receive Him as our personal Savior and be able to escape this "Sin Sick World." He loves each and every one of us, so much that He even gave us all free will's. But wow, did we mess that up!

I do have a lot more to tell you, about my second hospital visit, as well, but let's wait a few chapters, for now; OK? You will find that episode quite interesting as well. I'm telling you these stories her now, because they are about the only thing that isn't documented by one of two police departments and a huge traumatic hospital.

None of it is "made up or exaggerated," but totally accurate and true.

Chapter Two

What's an "In (en) cumbent," to do?

H old your beans! No, I don't want to pepper you, or even salt you with questions or squash what I am about to explain here. But as you will see, this is really quite corny, but "plant" your thoughts on what I am asking about. Cucumbers might get pickled, or just stay fresh and raw. I am using words such as that, in order to make a clear point. Like so many other word in the English language, the only thing a person can do to properly define the actual meaning of that word is to know the context and sometimes to just hope that they are assuming the correct meaning. The author rarely tells you that the word is being used as noun, or adjective or verb. They (authors) *expect that You* get to the point of what they are trying to say, which leaves the reader required to surmise the correct definition.

Just look at the "headlines" of a newspaper or magazine. Rarely do the huge print words really mean what the article is trying to say. It is just a teaser_ to get you to read further.

The presenter is then specifically using certain other words to clarify or seemingly emphasize what they are saying. Did you know that the dictionaries don't even know for sure or agree with each other as to exactly how to spell this word? Does it start with the letter (i) or (e) as this causes me to be bound to tell you that "It felt encumbered upon me to present this information that I am about to share with you, prior to the completion of the whole Doppelganger saga.

So please let me continue. To begin with; any one of you who have learned some other language, other than English, will most likely agree with me, in my saying that the English language is "terribly insufficient in its grammatical accuracy and correctness. For a quick example; the word encumber is only accurate in the reader or hears understanding of the context it is presented in, and at the time of its reading. Why do you think that there are (so many) translations of the Holy Bible? They're not trying to "re-interpret it, but rather make it more understandable to current generations. How many of us say *thy, thou, thee.* No one that know. I shared in my last book that the King James English, just doesn't sound right to us anymore. Remember I told you readers about the Greek *Aorist* tense. We; in English don't even have a tense for those Greek words. It is defined as expressing the "past-present-and future in one word." What were the King James translators to do? Concoct the word "*hath*." Starting to get my point?

What's it meant? To be a *HOMOPHONE*

As I have been blessed to be a public school substitute teacher now in these last five years. I deal with this linguistic calamity on a daily basis. One of our English professors at Concordia High, put it like this. "For almost every {rule} in this language, there usually more exceptions. Example is, "I before E except after C." Here is the dictionary definition of the word that a clear paradigm of what I am trying to convey. I am *Not* doing this to excuse any "grammatical" errors that you find in this text. But by now, you probably realized that I have finally overcome my fear of a poor grade from my English/Grammar teacher. And YES I do use "Spell-Check." The European "rule" is just the opposite of the American rule; as to where to put the period or question mark before or after the quotes. Here in the U.S. it is supposed to be in front; yet in the United Kingdom English, it comes after the quotes.

You are going to have to accept (hopefully) my ingratiating use of the word *onomatopoeia*. Which simply means: "Origin: noun

1. the formation of a word, as *cuckoo, meow, honk,* or *boom,* by imitation of a sound made by or associated with its referent. "Now; wasn't that *juicy.* Or *sizzling* with explanation; right from the dictionary itself.

Maybe this is all coming from my "left-handed" "only child" character again? The value behind all of this is to enforce my point of how it is so important to know what you are believing. Here is just one example that I am trying to show you.

So sorry…English teachers and grammataticians. {Is that even a word?}

Incumbent:
"Adjective:
1. holding an indicated position, role, office, etc., currently: the incumbent officers of the club.

2. obligatory (often followed by on or upon):
    a duty incumbent upon me.
3. Archaic. Resting, lying, leaning, or pressing on something:
    "incumbent upon the cool grass."

Noun:

4. the holder of an office: The incumbent was challenged by
    a fusion candidate."
5. *British*. a person who holds an ecclesiastical benefice.

Then there is the same word pronounced the same way and
actually has a whole different meaning. Just the pronunciation
may end up being so deceiving. Here is a *homophone*.

In-cumber: used with object
"verb: (used with object)

1. to impede or hinder; hamper; retard:
    Red tape encumbers all our attempts at action.
2. to block up or fill with what is obstructive or superfluous:
    a mind encumbered with trivial and useless information.
3. to burden or weigh down:
    She was encumbered with a suitcase and several packages.
4. to burden with obligations, debt, etc.
    Expand: a less common spelling t encumber
    "So which one is correct which one means which. {My
    point; exactly}

Also," encumber". Even sounds real similar...doesn't it?
Yes! I just did a "cut and Paste" thing to what you just read.
Straight from the "hallowed" dictionaries of old Oxford, Webster

etc. It truly seems almost for sure that this is one of the better reason's God chose the Bible to be written in Hebrew (Old Testament) and then in Greek (New Testament). Basically because they have so many words and spelling differences to clarify the accuracy of what is trying to be conveyed? So in "other words" ha ha. I have found it imperative to tell you before we proceed to this story that, so much was expedited. I learned in Greek class, years ago that clear example, which is right here.

LOVE:

Agape: "unconditional" (God's love for mankind John 3:16)

Phileo: "brotherly love" (Philadelphia)

Eros: "romantic"erotic (usually physical)

Storge: "natural affection" (love of a parent, or child)

Epithomia: "Strong desire of any kind" (usually lust)

And OUR One single English word for each of these various definitions, is LOVE. That's It. I know I shared some of this in the other book; but the significance is that important to me. I'm trying to reinforce another example of the Bible's validity.

The "<u>DOA Who Made It</u>" occurrence was initiated on July 1st 1986. The Doppelganger incident took place (as I have been saying) in the middle of March on a Wednesday afternoon/ evening 1992, prior to "daylight-savings." That was just three months shy of a full six years later. It is imperative (not incumbent ha-ha) to tell you of some of the "benevolent" activities that transpire, leading to my authorship of this read.

CAP IT OFF!

Here now, in my life's story, post (meaning after) {not a fence-*post*}, "<u>The DOA Who Made It;</u>" yet prior to my commencing to write this book <u>"The Doppelganger Did It.</u>" There have been so many unimaginable or literally impossible type occurrences, truly that neither one individual nor a group of people, (as you will clearly see soon) could have performed these event.

I do truly find it significantly important to share these, as to verify or validate even more, both of my books; now, which I have just listed. Reading one or two stories like these, your only real conclusion of what these two are both saying is that as these "action adventures" must be just "made Up" Sorry...As difficult as it may be, to accept from one individual; please know that They are both very true, and very real.

Presented before, is the fact that numerous people around me in my life, repeatedly have told me that I must write a book of all these "miraculous" activities. Not disposing of the idea, I have never wanted to inflate myself, or become "outstanding" in my person. And yes now having read the first portion of this soon to be best seller, and then if you have read my first book. An individual could easily say "How can you honestly say such a thing?"

I must have "contributed" to these words and descriptive details. No! Not one bit. There is no opacity to my words. The veracity is so important to me and my true main goal in writing these two books, is to ultimately give God the glory and honor for what has taken place in my life and body. Accolades simply cannot go anywhere else but to HIM!

I know, some of you were waiting to see, "just what is his real motive? Is it simply to make money writing some unique and interesting books; that is "most likely" destined to become a movie? (Ala publisher) Or is Dave just trying to scare people into always wearing a helmet when they are driving or riding, let's say a motorcycle, bicycle, ATV's, or a dirt-bikes, or even if they find themselves in other potentially hazardous, activities, such as sky diving or even bungee jumping. Despite what we guys like to arrogantly think of ourselves; we must admit that the human body, is actually quite "frail", to withstand some of the abuse we put it through. AND...besides all of that, I have to share something that I don't think has been copy written or trademarked; but here is probably the best way to summarize most of us "fella's." 'What's the difference between U.S. Savings Bonds, and men? Answer.... "Savings Bonds Mature."

I find it so "blasphemously" wrong for an adult to make a child wear a helmet (state law or not), but they see no need to have one on themselves. Do they sincerely believe that upon an occurrence, they will always be OK? Do their heads grow so much thicker or stronger? Please. But their passengers won't ride without a helmet on. Therefore displaying the validity of having a helmet to be worn. Just a modicum of common sense dictates that "what's good for the goose is good for the gander; (bet ya haven't heard that one in a while, right?)

So how can that type of person; turn around and say that helmets "really aren't safe." Is that why they have a loved one wear one? While putting it on a child's head, do they say "This thing really isn't going to help you but, you better put it on anyway?" Reeaally.... See why I used such a big word for all that? Guys!

Would you expect your favorite football or hockey player, to go out on the field or ice with NO helmet on? Of course not! How absurd.

Book 'em "Dano"

Now in the early to mid part of the twenty-first century; it was mid-day in the end of January. I was sitting at home nursing my right shoulder that I was still in much pain with. See, this had been my second rotator cuff surgery, which I needed to have done in the last six years. The surgical procedure that I had in early December had been caused months earlier in late fall, when I was helping my now very very senior father remove his pier from the lake shore where he and my mom had lived {and me as a child & adolescent} for now over 55 years. NO it didn't happen on a motorcycle!

Here I am, (again) in late January of the new year 2013; I was "nursing" that poor shoulder, awe; when the telephone rang, and it was a representative from a publisher, who was calling to asked me about writing a book regarding my "very interesting" life history. I asked him just where he had gotten my name from and what did he know about my dramatic life?

He said that it was from someone who knew me well. But he didn't know their name. He asked me to tell him a little bit and after a few statements, we talked for over an hour and a half that day. He listened quite intently, then he insistently convinced me to write a book about the whole thing. Now this is a new revelation to me; when I said "so you want me to write an autobiography, no?" "No!" He insisted, "It is now known as a

{Personal Testimony,} no longer an autobiography." "Really?" I popped back. "Yup, that is what their now called." He assured me. So after giving him a synopsis about most of my years on this earth, I must have even convinced myself, so that I finally, after all of these years since, should get to putting it all down on paper. But then... I told him of my second incident. {This book's main story event}. Which after "blowing him away," with all of these "miraculous" occurrences, I asked him, if I shouldn't put both stories in the book.

"Absolutely NOT-Don't You Dare!" he briskly snapped back. "If your first story becomes anywhere near as popular as we are sure it will. You better have another book coming." So my next question to him then was; "does that mean I am going to have to keep having more {accidents} just so I can keep writing more books?" NOooo! Was his regretful response. All that I could say was "whew thanks." Your readers will be "demanding," more; He said again." Oh"...was all I could say.

In a rather reluctant sort of manor, they (the publisher) finally convinced me in a de facto format, to get started at writing the book, which has since, as many of you know became <u>The DOA Who Made It!</u> Here again, now being the last day of January, I said to myself "self..." {Good thing, that's all that I called myself...huh?} I hate it when I say "huh." Anyway I still could type with my one arm in a sling. It did look pretty funny though. And you guessed it; I certainly did now have the time. Then I sat down and wrote the title first; (good thing for that too-no?) <u>The DOA Who Made It!</u> I didn't contrive that for a way of naming my story. Rather, despite all of my degrees, and certifications, that title was awarded to me by the medical staff of the hospital where I found myself, being put, now so frequently, as a "border" of sorts. And I will loudly proclaim that it certainly wasn't my preference; especially with the annexed pain, which always coincided with it.

The reason that I am informing you (hopefully you're the reader,) of this ancillary information is, because it truly isn't insignificant at all. OK! I will preface this with the fact that I was and still am quite "stupid" uneducated about the whole publishing industry itself. You say to yourself "self" Soo. Likely, you're now as really confused as I am.

I started trying to place some form of manuscript, onto my laptop, and by mid-March, I had even gotten twenty some pages done. Now getting closer to the end of May, the publisher informed me that I needed to send in the first fifteen pages or so, and they would "double-check" it for approval. "Approval, what kind of approval?" I did live that life and had that "death" experience. I had then come to find out that the publisher had such high standards in their printing, that they would not print anything less than very "pure and moral text. That's fine I said, this is just <u>my true life</u> story, there won't be any cuss words, or sex talked about. Sol I expected everything to be fine...I said. Boy was I was WRONG!

"Bloody" well *<u>Write</u>*?

Several days after I had sent in the first few chapters, I got an e-mail telling me that they were so sorry, but they could<u> Not</u> publish my book, because it didn't meet up to their standards.

"What?" was my only response (back to myself again). "What's wrong with it?" Who knows my life story better than I do?" I promptly called the representative and queried just what was going on; that they couldn't publish my book? We are sorry Dave, but you used the word 'blood" in it, several times even, already and we "Will Not" publish anything with that word, unless it is in a direct Bible quote. All I could say was "You've got to be kidding." I was just describing some of the seemingly "misadventures" of life that either I had encountered, or took place to somebody else.

So; instead of "juicing" it up to draw more readers, I had to "tone everything down." So if you are one of the large collection of reader, all I can say is "I'm sorry-that I wasn't able to make it as {graphic} as I felt it needed to be in places. However I will say that I have been complemented on the book; a great deal of times. Thank You! All !

So now thinking that I have been fully accepted, all I had to do was finish it, and send it off to be printed. Boy was I ever wrong. Here we are in mid-June, and it's almost done. I called the publisher and they then informed me that I had to write a "back cover, and an inside front flap and back flap, for the hard cover version. "Ok; I guess." Was my response, but please let me tell you that putting all of the information in a small cavity of space is kind of tough. But I got through it, and sent it in the end of June; then they called me and said that I had to submit samples and work with the art department to make the cover.

With my love for art and drawing that seemed quite appealing to me. I'll say this, that the ideas, and concepts that I sketched were fun, but not very professional. Their art department and

I spent a lot of time testing different ideas. Then it suddenly occurred to me (yes...things do take me awhile to catch on) I had numerous black and white photographs in my records that the city of Franklin Police department had taken at the "accident." The front cover is one of them. Hurray! The art department was all over it, so we "manufactured a background with the tombstone and blank desert background. They wanted that, so as not to take away from the predominance of the cycle and car. Oh; and by the way, there isn't a cemetery right there either, I just needed that there. It wasn't their fault on "that one." Hey com'on; I thought that "RIP Not Yet" was pretty fitting and cool. By the way; if anyone cares, about the motorcycle in the picture, that I had just been extracted from, had a huge whopping <u>161</u> miles on it in total. That was It!

I haven't said anything; so far. "Really? So what is this all been?" NO, NO. Please quit "butting in" OK? THERE! Now, please just keep reading. Almost immediately after I had started the book, it came to me that I would have about a hundred and fifty thousand, extra pair of eyes in Milwaukee, Wisconsin in late August for "somebody's" 110th birthday celebration. It has been known to bring quite a few motorcyclists from all over the world.

I "gently" mentioned and inferred frequently, while conversing with the publishing company, that I "needed" the book to be "out" by at least August 16th. That insistence, as far as I knew was really "cutting IT, tight." We did get the whole thing ready to go in late July. When I sent in the manuscript and approvals for all of the art work. I let them know it Again, August 16th! No one there, had the audacity to say "lotsa luck" on that one, but I could almost hear them chortling on that. Well, Believe it or NOT! On August 16th that book was electronically ready for sale. That meant that I could now begin advertising it, since it is now available to customers; the printed version would take just a little longer, to get out.

"Small" Miracle #1 Complete! & Released

As I have said, I love to do marketing and promotions, so I contacted a Billboard company that I had dealt with years earlier. They had one spot left on an electronic board everyone would see coming into Milwaukee. {hmph good idea?} Let's see. I called and was connected with a sales rep that I had never had any contact with prior. His name was Rob B. (he knows who he is) I see him as part of my "Benevolence miracle worker status" Keep reading- You'll see. This is so cool

Considering the idea of advertising the book during this massive show; whenever I was not working on the book in early July, I called the billboard company, and found out the information, on size, run, cost, etc. They made a few samples and I kept telling them what I wanted to see on it, but all they kept saying to me was, sorry that "wouldn't work". Another thing, I had no knowledge of, was that the electronic billboard shared by several others advertisers like myself, (No not other book authors silly) would stay up for eight seconds at a time; twenty-four hours a day, seven days a week. In other words it meant that each time my ad would show, it would be up over 5600 times a day. That sounds like a lot! NO? I needed the board to be up for the whole week of the birthday celebration. Yes they could arrange that. Rob told me that they had [1] spot left (hm-hm again) so we got all of the business dealings taken care of, but I could not have it up until the 16th or the actual release of the book.

Board Yet

The 16th of August, happened to be a Friday, when it could start displaying the book. Rob, the billboard company's sales rep., called me to say that "everything" was all set. Now he would just have to e-mail me the contract to sign multiple times and even initial several spots that he would highlight. "Send it over." I replied. Dave I will need it in hard copy (paper form) before I can put it up. OK. I'll run it over. It came to my computer, but the problem was that I was unable to print it on the brand new printer that I had recently gotten. I had "Windows 8 and the printer wasn't set for that. So "Now What?"

I called Rob and informed him of my dilemma. "Dave...I can't put it up `till it has all been signed. Here comes One more "NOW WHAT?" I strongly urged him to please stay a little past five, and I would be there to sign all of those papers, right there and then. Fortunately enough, he agree.

I won't be backing up to far here, but I have to share a little bit more of what took place prior to all of this. It shows how all of these occurrences had to be in place {just right}. A week or so before all of these conditions, I had an idea. (in quotes?) "Why shouldn't I take the picture of the cover of the book, and get four printed out on a page of post card stock, and use them as hand-outs?" Hoping that may be beneficial to the "cause," I went over to the office supply store that I use a lot. There is a young man named Jessie who worked there, and he seemed to be able to help in any way, and boy did he become a big blessing for me and my projects. So he made sure that they were able to print up a hundred pages, for me, and quite quickly. Problem was I needed to pick them up this Thursday afternoon at the latest, and proceed to use them in another format that I'll tell you about shortly.

So I hopped on one of my motorcycles and shot over to the office supply store, and saw the postcard size book covers and a short "teaser" script on the back. They had cut each page into fourths, like I had planned. Everything looked great; so I thanked the girl, for getting them done by today {Friday] she had done them so well. I paid the bill and got on my bike and headed over as fast as I could, to the billboard company ASAP!

This is where it starts to get real interesting, (if it hasn't been already?) I arrived about five after five, (five pm is their closing time) Rob was waiting for me as was his pretty young secretary/receptionist. I wasn't too sure if I saw steam coming from her nose, but I sure knew she didn't want to be in that office on an August Friday afternoon. Just standing behind Rob, her demeanor wasn't improving to say the least. Her light summer frock wasn't able to improve her presence. She was overly anxious, and wanting to be doing something far more enjoyable, and most definitely somewhere else on the start of a warm hot summer eve. But even her "well done "make-up could *Not* hide her "distain" for my lateness. Rob however, welcomed me in to the office and to approach her desk. She needed to show me all of the places to sign and initial. I went to the desk and kept following her long nailed finger motions. I hadn't finished the last signature, while she was rapidly on her way out the door.

Rob handed all of my copies to me while he too, was earnestly escorting me to the door. My motorcycle was sitting almost immediately in front of it, and so we both said good night to each other. I then heard the lock click, and I started putting my helmet on. Just then, it dawned on me. "Duh! Why didn't I give him a few of my new book cover postcards? (I now had 400 of them in my cycle) so he could share them with people in his life, friends, family co-workers; but probably not his secretary? At that point, (so typical of me, to-late of course). I thought I'll leave three or four of the cards, and he could, being a salesman and all, maybe give them to others that he meets or knows. Oh was I wrong!

I quickly ejected myself off the cycle, and started tapping on the door; to no avail. "Darn" I thought. Wait, I'll put a few between the cracks of the door jam. If they fall out he'll know what's going on when he comes out to his car. Just as I had put them in the slight separation, and was putting my helmet back on, now for the second time. He came and opened the door as the cards all fell to the pavement. I bent over and retrieved and then handed them over his way and said that I had just gotten them printed, and maybe he could pass them around. This is where it get s really awesome.

"It" showed that it was rather imperative for him to be leaving work as well, but he looked at the book cover cards, and said "How many of these do you have, with you?" I told him that I had just picked them up from the printer and in the paper bag I now had 400 hundred in there, all precut and ready to go. His next comment floored me. He insisted "Give them all to me! I'll be working the whole birthday party at all of the multiple venue events scattered around the Milwaukee area for this huge weekend. The corporate office and plant, the Lake Michigan Park, the State Fair Park, and all over, where thousands and thousands would be gathering. "Dave, I am working all of the locations the whole weekend." "Really?" was all I could conjure up to say at that offer.

Handing them over to him quickly, I repeated my appreciation over and over again, as he was re-locking his front door. I simply left, "REJOICING." Please realize that there is "NO WAY in (down-there)" that anybody even with deep pockets like maybe some huge company could afford to pay to get that kind of "personal interaction" with a world-wide audience of cyclists, to be handed my book cover cards. It would be seen as a business venture and another motorcycle company would NOT tolerate it. But that's how it happened. If that isn't incredible.

"Small" Miracle #2 Complete!

Guess where I drove my cycle to, right after that occurrence? Yup, back to the office supply printer. "Please make another huge group of book covers." I begged. She didn't have a problem with the order, but how quick, really mattered. They were all done the next day. Clearly you know why she gets all my office equipment business. Here is what they all looked like. Good thing they all looked the same too, hey?

You sure Can "BANK" On This One

My wife and I have been banking at the same big national bank ever since we were married back in 1973. We had seen a lot of employees come and go over the years, but this last group has been around now for a good while.

The manager was a very energetic gal. One can see her medium length very brunette hair behind her perpetual smile, get around that facility in an urgently thorough manor. That being said, a couple of years ago, she and I had a business arrangement (somewhat outside of the bank business). I was working for an old acquaintance and his brother. They owned several new car dealerships, and they now sought to "branch out" into the motor-cycle business. They had just taken on the Triumph Motorcycle franchise and they asked me to get "IT" up and running for them. They also took on a franchise of Chinese ATVs'/UTVs'.

That all being said. Back to the bank manager. The main highway that the bank, and one of the new car (Subaru) dealer-ships was on, which was where the new Triumph dealership was also located, and then besides, just four miles further south was my Kawasaki/Oak Creek MotorSports dealership which were all attached this big main road, it is simply known to the locals as 27th St. which passing all the way from Marquette Michigan, to Miami Florida, is also known as the U.S. 41.

Trying to conjure up the nostalgic feeling of "Old U.S. 41, like "Route 66. A good number of businesses wanted to, shortly after there was a huge Upgrade to that national highway, which of course went right past all of these business. They had all sorts of community activities, with street parties, and a whole carnival atmosphere, for much of that summer.

They approached me one day, while I was in the bank, and asked if I knew of a good raffle ticket award. "Just so happens, I do". I readily assured them. "How about a really nice ATV?" After a couple of days they called me, at the dealership, asking for more information. I shared with them all of the necessary details; then two days later, they said "OK...Let's do IT. All went well, with that whole event and giveaway.

Now back to the postcard style book cover cards. I had gone back to the Office supply store, who had made those postcards up for me, and bought another huge packet of them. On my way home, I stopped at the bank, to get some change.

Completely unaware, at that particular time, I said "hi' to that female bank manager and shared a little bit of the amazing opportunity that had just taken place with the billboard rep. which had just come Out of "NO WHERE,"

She then piped up with "Dave, do have any more of those cards?" "Funny you should ask." I replied. "I was just at the office supply store and picked up hundreds more, and besides all of that, I just received four hundred {cycle pucks!}." "Wwhaat?" came out of her mouth, simultaneously to her very eerie expression.

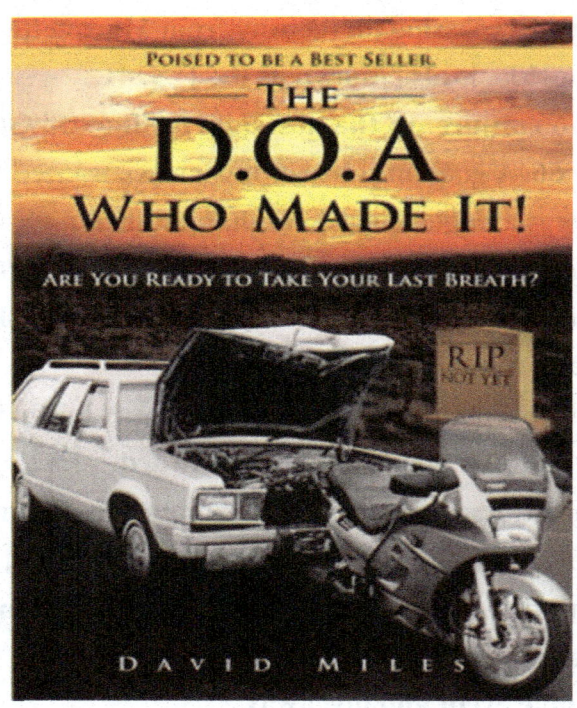

"Here, I have one. Check this out. Cyclists love 'em. When you put your side stand down to park, but the ground is soft or muddy, this three or four inch plastic disc gives your bike a lot more support security to not fall over. She immediately came back with. "Could we use these cycle pucks with your postcards, and hand them out to the cycle riders that come to get a patch, and a stamp for their {poker run} type event for all over the city?" I somehow brought myself to naturally say "Sure!"

There goes a few hundred more, and the cycle pucks, came in a nice purple with white lettering that said "<u>The DOA Who Made It!</u>" (Surprise! Who would-a guessed?)

Small Miracle #3 complete

Now admit with me "Isn't GOD Awesome? Really how else? Absolutely NONE of this could "just have happened" like that over and over again, by means of "fate or good luck." To simply repeat something like "oh what a coincidence," or isn't that some stroke of luck? Huh?"

For such an educated and well learned society like we have these days; why is it the only answer to occurrences like that are "that was just good luck" Really, that is our supposed wise and well thought through answer. Even you, have to admit how weak that is.

Really? You're the kind of reader who would just dilute so many activities of life to those rather 'meaningless" words? Please don't do that to yourself. There has to be a better conclusive answer to things like that.

Else what do people like that have to "hang on to?.

Morals?

Values?

Honesty?

Peace & security?

None of those have any significance to a person who has no founding anchors in life.

How can anyone have arrogance or strength to "stand"; and on what principles? My Favorite, **is especially by those who are so (wise, spiritually and emotionally, psychologically,) that** *"it's just* <u>meant</u> **to be!" So I ask "So who meant- it-anyway?" another hmmmmm**

Chapter Three

Before "It" comes Back, At Us Again

Let's see…Where the PAST Has Been this time

The inland lakes of southeast Wisconsin are all beautiful, fresh, and often-times so much fun; be it with boats, swimming, fishing, "Jet Skiing" or just plain splashing in the gorgeous sandy settings they're found in. Some of us, even like it when they are froze over, so ice-fishing or ice-skating can be part of the winter joy. With the right conditions (thickness of the ice of course) some even brave the temperatures and go snowmobiling to and from different land bridges to the next lake. Life in those setting's was and is, so comfortable, and peaceful and sincerely downright enjoyable.

That's where and how I was raised back in the '50's and '60's. Being an only child had little effect on my enjoyment of life. I must confess though, I wasn't "big" on ice-fishing, even though I had attempted it more than several times. I figured those "poor" fish could use a break, after all even below the foot or more deep ice-pack, they still had to try to stay alive in that fridge cold water. Just how they're able to survive those temperature sure was something to try to comprehend.

If you want to see some of what I'll call, "God's handiwork" just stand on the east or west shore and watch a sunrise, or sunset, with the multi-colored fall leaves and the burning orange/yellow/red backdrop of the sun; with a few high clouds. If you are the kind of person that might think, "That's just how it has evolved." You have my pity, as certainly a person like that simply can't be a believer in much of anything. You might as well be color-blind then.

You'll never believe this…No?

But wait, YOU MUST be a believer in something, like…"I believe that this stop-light will change to green {someday-soon}. I believe that spring will really get here soon! I believe that the sun will shine {any day now}. I believe my employer will give me a pay-check (of some sort-now days be it paper or electronic) Etc. See, YOU really DO have to Believe!

Let's say that you truly were some sort of "non-believer' you wouldn't be able to wait for your paycheck to come. Or your birthday to happen. Or your tax return, to arrive. My point is that we all have to believe in {somebody or something} whether we want to like it or not.

How could you genuinely partake in any form of an honorarium, say for the military, or a departed friend or relative? Wouldn't you just have to say "they're gone so what, that's it." I can only say," How sad.

What's the point of "so-many people like presidents for instance? Who want to have a *"Legacy."* If we are just *gone;* what's the point for value in retaining a memory of the departed?

Where does "concern for others" even come from then? I mean like maybe the thousands and thousands of missionaries, world-wide? Or even the "Peace Core, or "Doctors without Borders? And where did things like...Sympathy, fear, guilt, worry, doubt, came from where?

If we are so "busy" advancing ourselves with the mentality of only "the strong will survive" Just where could those conditions have come from over the so-called billions of years of evolution? So why do we have names on tombstones, too? Isn't the pizza one enough?

As a young boy (an only child, remember) living by the lake {quite by myself Ok I let my parents in to,} I came to learn that I had to believe mom and dad would be coming home soon; after I got home from school. And I had to believe that my dog (who bit everybody,) wouldn't bite me. And that my sand-box would provide me with much entertainment.

My early years growing up were pretty sedentary. I guess you could call my formative years, somewhat and seemingly quiet, except for all of the different "death incidents" that I was exposed to at such a young age. I had a rather great family life, even though I was pretty much by myself as a child. Living out in the country-side about some twenty miles from the Milwaukee Wisconsin area, where the most exciting part of life for me, was that all of my many hours, days, and weeks, were spent swimming in the pretty little lake that my parents lived on. (No... not a houseboat). Yes, I could have gotten in big trouble while swimming out to a very large raft, that was anchored way out in the deep water, which was about 15 feet where they had it anchored. I would dive down as far as I could go, to the anchors (concrete filled fifty five gallon oil drums) that held the raft in place. "They" say it was about twenty some feet down, but I was just glad to hit the top of those big barrels. No snorkel, no air tanks. I would just take a few deep breaths and down I went, 'till I reached the heavy chain hooks. I kept challenging myself to see how long I could hold my breath, and stay down there.

To *bee* or <u>Not</u> to BE

Then one day, while I was still little; I went outside and sat on a corner of my nice little playtime sandbox. When I noticed that there was a strange hole in the sand and it seemed to go way down into the ground quite a ways below the sand. I hadn't played in the sandbox for some time, say maybe a week or so.

Being a young curious boy, I decided to explore this hole, that I hadn't put there, but none the less, there it was, about the size of maybe a quarter or so! I decided to venture into that hole with one of my plastic toy soldier's (WWII) head first, then another and another.

When suddenly some of the soldiers were coming back up & out of the hole! What's going on here I fearfully questioned to myself? Then to my startling surprise out from behind the toy soldiers came a huge swarm of wasps; with such a loud buzz and sporadic flying around, all I could do was jump up and flaill my arms and runaway as fast as I could.

I shortly realized that I just couldn't outrun, or zig-zag, or flail my arms or scream, enough to keep from getting repeatedly stung all over my body. Crying/screaming sure came out of my mouth and rather quite loudly I might admit.

Yes, my belief in the fun and safety of my sand-box respite, couldn't be relied upon anymore. All that I could do was bewail and scream to my highest pitch and cry simultaneously. "Mom-Mom! Help! Help!" Miss-belief is as bad as dis-belief. Both are going to be less that what you may expect. Here in the various, little segments of life and beyond. Yes I say "beyond" because, it's there and coming to all of us. Sooner or later; let's face it. I know what I say because, (as my first book clearly qualifies) I have been there.

"Can You Hear the Train Coming?" YES It IS coming! There is *Nothing* surreptitious about it. Just try to picture a huge freight train coming right at you straight down the tracks. You see a very little dark dot…way, way down the track, but how far away is it really? And how fast is it coming directly at you? And, it looks like there are so many cars attached behind that engine, but just "how many are there? (Say that each car is another year of your life?) Staying on the track; means you're staying alive, but just for "how long?" Each car is a little different than the other, another chapter in your life, but again "how many cars are there left? Will it de-rail, before it gets here? Interesting questions to ask oneself. Will the last car, arrive and then go by, before you were expecting it too? Just get my point?

Despite all of the "so-called" experts, that don't want to have to deal with conscience, and morals/ethics. Deep in your heart, you have to know that YOU ARE more than "Dust in the Wind," and that your life really does have significance, to somebody other than yourself and maybe your relatives and friends.

Of course, as we get older and get married, and have kids, and then someday grandkids, we put a lot of our faith in our relevance to life. But "then What?" Important people like to leave their legacy, in say a building, or concept, or maybe a social change. So if a devout atheist or evolutionst want to leave a legacy; "what for?" What value is there?

The big *STING*

Alright...I'll get back to the bees. I really didn't know if they were bees, or wasps or hornets. Hearing me screaming; my mother came running out of the back door, which was closest to the kitchen and sand-box. She realized what had just happened and tried diverting herself from the swarm, and scrambled towards me. When she saw and heard the stinging hoard, she slowed down, so as not to get them chasing her too.

Finally we got down towards the end of the long flat yard, and most of the (bees-wasps-hornets) were gone. I just fell on the grass and cried and scratched all over. From head to toe, my body was riddled with bright red pock marks. My mom kept trying to tell me to stop scratching them but I just couldn't. I needed some form of relief. That's one railroad car I wouldn't want to visit again.

As I shared in the last book, my mom worked for a family doctor, and she knew how to make up some kind of "paste" she quickly ran and made some up, and brought it out to me on the grass. She smeared it everywhere she could see stings. But I had also gotten "a bunch" of those horrible stings up my shorts and those blistering bites really burned a lot, all over my groin and butt.

It did take some time for me to get back into trusting the comfort and joy of my beloved sand-box again, but I learned to accept and appreciate it for all of its enjoyable past time it gave to me. But I must tell you; that I did learn to check the sand for large vertical holes.

Once the weather warmed up enough to go swimming, I was usually found in one of two places, either in bed or in the lake. That swim beach next door with that great big huge swimmers raft was almost my "home away from home," for the summer.

Something' *fishy*... Is going on

Once I finally got old enough to go to Kindergarten, I thought "here we go now". Only problem was Lake DeNoon didn't have any kind of kindergarten; so my parents decided to send me to my mother's parent's house. It was about 10 miles away in a nice small twn a little closer to Milwaukee. It was and still is known as Hales Corners. This was a much bigger and busier town than Muskego where Lake DeNoon is situated. They even had street-cars and city buses...WOW! There was a great big tavern/bar/restaurant /rooming house, right there in the middle of town and across the street from my Grandparents house, that they built right downtown. My mom's father was born in 1903, so he was too young to go into World War 1, and then they (the military) said that he was too old to join in World War II.

My grandpa, on my mom's side, whose house I stayed at for kindergarten, would go out to the lake with me and some-times grandma, to go fishing. He did that throughout the whole summer time, so I got to see my parents.

But starting in late April or early May, (depending how the spring season was going) we would go "spawn" fishing for "pan fish." That was an absolute, {WOW!} Cane poles, and a coffee can filled with dirt and a huge load of freshly dug up; worms, from grandpa's special cache of red-worms and big night crawlers. We would row his fishing boat out to the drop off, directly in front of my parents' house. Because the water was so clear you could see where the sand stopped and the sea weeds started. Right on the edge were the fish beds. You could see circles down on the floor of the lake. We would put a worm on the hook, drop it in, let it sink and grab the pole, because a fish just took it, and started swimming off rapidly.

The males were busy down there fanning the soft sand to make a placed for the females to lay their eggs. They wanted *nothing* to drift over their bed, so if a piece of sea-weed, or maybe a leaf would come sinking down over their bed, they just snapped it hard. Being uninterested in eating the worm, they just wanted it out of their way. Boy, would those blue gill's and crappie, and even some perch tug hard, pull, and really fight to get off that hook and line.

In about an hour before the setting sun, my grandparents and I would catch twenty or thirty nice big fish. They filled a good size pail. What was really neat to see, was after the females laid their eggs; when you would look down into the clear water. From seven to eight feet above, from the boat, it looked just like a huge array of fried eggs, down in the water. The males had made the beds so smooth with fine stones, and sand they looked close to white, that with the bright yellow eggs in the middle, one sure got hungry for a fried egg.

Here is where it got a little more difficult. When we reached shore and tied the boat to the pier. We would bring the life vests, and oars, on to shore, with our catch. Then we would go over to the picnic table and lay some old newspaper on the table surface and start "cleaning" the catch.

My grandpa taught me how to clean pan fish real well. They were too small to fillet, compared to a big bass or walleye. {Who ever named a fish that?} Maybe someone who mounted it and could only see one eye on the wall?

The first thing you had to do was take a sharp paring knife and "scale" the fish, then cut it's head off {just right} and then gut it and clean it up. But if you have ever had a fried or grilled Blue-gill, and safely picked the bones off. You could hardly imagine a better meal. And the perch were even more delicious.

OK! All of you "vegetarians" can breathe again,

If or when I wasn't in the lake, I was conversing with the little old man who took the (believe this or not) dime from the potential swimmer, and then would stamp the hand of the person who wanted to go swim or just "plotch" in the lake. They could change their clothes, in a huge wooden building right by the shore. The male/female sides were separated into two separate areas. But you could step into a changing room (most still had just a curtain) and get your swimming suit on. Once you had your suit on and were ready "Out" you sprang into the bright sun light, and just pick a spot on the beach where you might simply put a blanket, as your "territory" on the soft white sand, which gave you a place to put you belongings. For another nickel you could get a big brass safety pin with an attached medallion that had a number stamped o it showing your cubicle basket that simply sat on an open shelf. That's all there was to it.

"With AGE comes Wisdom!" Really?

Finding out that I should plan on eventually become an adult, I thought that it might be advantageous to see what makes "it" work better to be one of them sooner or later. All of the "oldsters" were so "ready" to tell me everything that they knew, in life. If they had so much as a listening ear to my queries, they would go on to expound all of their knowledge, on me.

Now with that being said, I found myself talking with adults as much as I could, and not just try to act like the "little kid" that I was, but to be as "grown-up" as I could be. I figured that "hey that will be me someday too;" so I might see if I can get a "head start," on this whole thing they call adulthood

These folks all had lots of stories, and being as smart as I am (ha-ha). Like any fourth grader, I thought that I could differentiate which ones were, say real and true, and which ones were just a lot of "baloney". Boy...life sounded quite interesting if I ever get out of this little quiet country neighborhood.

However, even before all of that, I still had some *other* growing up to do. Because I needed a lot more developing, before I became this (oh..So..wise) nine year old. Aren't all nine year olds ready-mature, and fully developed (puberty?)

Grandpa was… Always trying to "Milk It"

Grandpa Irvin Ruehle, was one of quite a few of the "hand diggers (shovels)" of the septic lines that needed to come out from Milwaukee's sewage lines. I'm sure it would have been a lot safer than the war. But the ditch was two feet higher than even he was. Hey now look; for five bucks a day; it was worth the dig. I guess. But it was obviously real hard work for 10 hours a day with a shovel, then be up by five am, to go back to the milk run, with the big truck, off to the various different farms, to pick up cans of milk.

He was a very tall individual for his generation, six foot three inches, and he had arm strength like you couldn't imagine. He started out in the nineteen thirties driving a large box truck seven days a week, to many different farms around Southeast Wisconsin and he would pick up their milk, to take to the dairy, back in the city. For decades that task was accomplished by heaving full and very heavy milk cans up into the truck, then drive back into the city of Milwaukee, and drop those cans off at the dairy. After that, he would have to pick up the washed out empties and return them to the farmers the next day while getting their very heavy full can-loads of milk. You just couldn't take a day off, because the cows gave their milk, each and every day, be it a Saturday, Sunday or holiday, clearly the cows didn't care while they were lactating, the milk had to go somewhere. For his last fifteen years or so, he advanced along with the farmers and had a huge tanker truck that he would, take to the farm milk house, and extract the milk from that large behemoth steel that was in a special building near the cow barn. He would then drive back into the dairy, where they would just have to pump it out into the plants massive containers of milk to get homogenized and bottled to be delivered to the customer's house or apartment. Naturally, they had big rigs above the truck to "super cleanse" the inside of his truck, after empting each load. He even thoroughly washed the outside of the truck everyday as well.

It would just great, when I would get to ride along with him. The best part was lunch, really. My grandma would make our favorite sandwiches, each and every morning about five am or so. She would usually take two slices of rye bread, then she would take some of the bacon grease that was still in the breakfast pan, and put a knife size dollop of that now white tasty smear, and put it on the top slice and the bottom slice, with at least two big chunks of bacon in between. Yum! Yum. I bet all of you "health freaks" just loved reading that one; NO? Cholesterol? What Cholesterol?

Believe it or not, besides all of that work. My grandpa was one of the local fire department officers, he even became Fire Chief for his last many years on the force. I was told that a few years before I came on this earth, that they were still using horses to pull the water fire trucks. (Just to show you, how old I really must be). Yes they had to hand pump the water out of the tank fire-wagon to get the water on the fire.

Here is a picture of the first Fire House in Hales Corners, Wisconsin

Grandpa Irv had a nice apple orchard as well, it was behind the house and his truck garage. He really took care of a lot of things including those trees. He would spray them, to keep the bugs and worms out from eating them up. (It's good to wash you apples or at least wipe them off) before you take a bite. That spray was nasty. All I know is that it had lead in it....ewe

So when they would have their local fair days on the spring and summer weekends, we would sit out-side on the porch and line up bags and bags of apples to sell. We sure did sell a lot of apples each fall, and they were really sweet and crunchy.

Grandpa and Grandma's back yard had a steep hill going down to the neighbor which just happened to be a great big thousands of acres Milwaukee County Park. It was so full of trees and had a big lagoon, and it's very own waterfall. A person would think that they were out in the "north-woods" somewhere. I used to go down into the park and (I could even carry a knife when I turned eight) find wild asparagus growing, I would cut a whole hand full and bring up to grandma and that was our evening vegetables.

Then some nine years later, I found myself working at that very same "Whitnall Park" for two different summer breaks. First year there I worked up on in a small office above the reception building. Three very adult women and I were rather "stuffed" in there. I was sent to work there, because I had such good typing skill. (Remember I was a lefty). It just didn't sit well with me, so the second summer I requested to go out with the gardeners and or park workers. Everybody thought that I was "nuts", for giving up the nice air-conditioned office for the hot humid, mosquito infested grounds.

UP hill...both Ways...yup

When I started 1st grade, back at Lake DeNoon, it was in a two room school house that had all eight grades in those two rooms. No, I am NOT as old as Abe Lincoln...really. My last two years of grade school, I attended a rather large school with a teacher per grade. Each grade even had about twenty five kids per level, instead of twenty five for all each grades first through fourth downstairs, and fifth through eighth, upstairs. I elaborated a little bit more of that in my first book; but we did walk to school and, yes, it was up hill both ways. Sure. The hardest part was having to wear sandals in the snow. (Ha-ha)

While I was in eighth grade, I found my parents (not that I lost them) were "scared" that I would get pulled into the military and shoved to the front lines in the Vietnam conflict. And so, my high-school years were spent in a private religious high school/ junior college, it located close to downtown Milwaukee, Wisconsin. Most all of us high-school students lived in big three story dormitory building. We were attending an all-boys only ministerial school, which was about twenty miles north east of my parent's house was on the lake.

Call of The WILD?

To say the least; it wasn't my idea, rather my mom and dad, insisted that I go to one of the two Lutheran Ministerial Prep schools in southeast Wisconsin. They thought that I would likely be put in battle right after boot camp. It was also a junior college; which after we finished those six years, we could go all different directions in the Concordia system to finish our ministerial and teacher training interests. I continued on to Concordia Teachers College; now known as Concordia University of Chicago, of which after another two years, I graduated with my Bachelor's degree. From there I was supposed to expected to get a "call" from a church or school and I could end up almost anywhere in the country, having become a Lutheran church leader.

But lacking any real "calls" I remained in the Milwaukee area, and stayed at selling and servicing motorcycles and snowmobile.

It was pretty fun and I did learn a lot of mechanical principles along the way as well. I realized that big truck and car engines are still mechanically quite the same as all of the smaller engines we had in cycles, lawn-mowers, and all of the different service schools, that I attended, were very helpful as well.

I will say that my personal interest was really in the advertising-marketing-promotional, area of business. I think, that is why we were so successful at sales, for so many years. "Marketing I learned, was getting your "name out there" for as little or no money spent to do it. Whereas advertising would of course cost, but it usually pinpointed your market demographics, better.

And especially, you'll hear me say this again. We DID become *America's Largest* Kawasaki dealers, and one of the Midwest's largest Evinrude, Allis Chalmers and even Cushman dealers; because we worked HARD for the customer. We didn't work as hard to get them as a customer, but rather to keep them as "our customer." It really paid off, too. Because they are the ones who did the selling for us. They liked our recognition of them, our service for them, and we really expressed our appreciation for them.

People want and need both recognition and respect. If a customer came in the store driving an old "beater" or a crumby little old cycle; and they were now thinking of upgrading. The worst thing a sales person could do is [demean-criticize} their current ride. Unconsciously all that you are really saying to them is that they sure have bad taste- in vehicles. And you know that all that means is now what you are trying to sell them is not "good, right, or proper, either.

Just let that {sink in}. We don't have to use the exact words, to convey a message. Be careful, with what you say!

I am not sure just where I learned *this* concept, but there is a principle known as {MA} *Mental Awareness.* All of us hear things, especially someone talking or announcing something, but we really didn't *know* what they just said. No it wasn't because we didn't understand the words, rather we just didn't "pay attention." Example: walking through the fair park, and hearing a guy or a gal "barking" their wares; like cook pans, knives, or bowls. But did you really know what it was that they just said? Probably not.

So many sales people, that hawk autos, or appliances, or maybe furniture, just don't seem to "get it." Get it? Get What? The {right-way} to talk to a prospect so that they will have willingness to involve themselves in the product that the sales person is trying to convey.

YOU/WE all remember somebody important to us that influenced us dramatically and he probably don't remember their words as much as we remember their "presentation, enthusiasm, demeanor, facial expressions and body language.

I have been approached by numerous people either young/old, male/female, rich/poor, that tell me they really "love" what I have to say. Because I present it with so much *PASSION.*

Which means to me that they really did "hear what I have to say" about a topic. Here are some of my techniques that validate my success in conversing.

1. I look them straight in the eyes (eyes- be it more than one person)
2. I try to reference something that they might be close to or thinking about.
3. Question just how "that" must feel or be recognized

4. **Try to actually get them to personalize the thought process that I am using.**

Now this isn't by any means…exhaustive and it isn't the only way to (sell or present) something to another person. But you know what? It really DOES work and has for over 59 years for me.

You don't have to be a sales person. Maybe you are just trying to sell a wash machine on Craigslist or you are attempting to get a neighbor or friend to agree with your line of thinking.

I have almost NEVER had someone look at me with the old "glazed over eyes" look. You will find that your words (from your thoughts) will be much more significan.

Chapter Four

The Land of Confusion?

As I have already shared in more detail in the first book; my childhood and adolescence could be categorized as "rather somewhat" pretty normal, for an American boy raised in the upper Midwest. But now, that is as far as it goes. Hang on for the ride!

Yes, I did, share a lot of quite interesting stories in my first book, but believe it or not, I really do even have more. None of these are made up; they're all true and very real life. All I wanted was to be simply "plain & normal"…even just a typical person, living life the old traditional way. No such luck, for me; I guess

Every spring, summer and early fall day, I would get up and drive my Kawasaki into work from out at my parents' house on Lake Denoon. It was about seventeen miles or so, west of the cycle shop; and it was of course all on nice country roads. Man! Going to work on the bike out in the country was so sweet and fun; I enjoyed every day's ride, despite the humidity or cold temperatures.

Was all that? Just a Rehearsal?

Could that first calamitous mishap that I had personally experienced six years ago, have been a harbinger, to future events coming in my life? I would like to say "NOT" but hey, in my case, who's to say otherwise?

Literally killed by a "dead drunk" (the DEAD Killing the DEAD?- HBO? Maybe?) Besides all of that, it was on a bright hot sunny July first, while just sitting still, at a red light of a very busy intersection, and then to be enraptured into an almost exact duplicate scenario. It is beyond obvious endorsement by anyone's definition. It simply, is too hard to even imagine as being tenable. How many zeros would an "odds" maker, have to use to bet on that one?

Notwithstanding, the almost reproductive equivalent did occur just like it did over a half decade prior. Despite age, education, background, race, or religion "conventional" is NOT a word or concept any person in their right mind could even acquiesce to.

Like a typical reader, the conclusion of these replicating events can only be affirmed to "must be a coincidence," or it must have "Just so happened." But let's say maybe one similitude, but nine exact "clones," of one another all simultaneously? Please! Don't write it off in such a trite manner. Or be so insulting and say "That must have been just "YOUR Fate!" Pleessee_ Really.

One, or maybe two happenings that are completely exact, and even so much as identical, but now compound that to NINE at one time-six years later? How can that be? One asks. So now you see why I have been displaying some of the unique exploits that have encased my life.

I am going to call this major event in my life a "retronym." It is a relatively new word, which only came about in 1980. That is according to Merriam Webster dictionary. Microsoft Word program, doesn't even know it exists, either. "It has the meaning of a more distinct and particular superclass of words used in the past." It would be like saying "snail mail"

"Doppelganger" is/was the only word that I could find to distinguish these "life/death" events. I defy anybody to tell me the plausibility of anything like this happening, especially in such a long span of time.

So what did you expect me to name this book? The "Ultimate Coincidence?" Or "The Great Just So Happens?" I could have used the famous old phrase "Against All Odds." But that has already been taken; though it would have been quite fitting, I believe.

If you can bring yourself to finish this book, and to not have some of your own personal convictions challenged; then I guess my life's stories weren't too valuable after all, like I thought that they might be, for other people's sakes. But I do hope and pray that my experiences helped to enhance your life, and of course demise.

Another "BIG BANG" theory

I guess you could say, I really did make a "Hit" with someone. See how words can have so many meanings. Please study the words before making your judgment's in life.

With a deadly horrifying glance, I instantly observed this, shall we say "very senior woman's" head, blindingly turn right towards me, in a blistering pivot while simultaneously showing a frightening expression of horror and panic, on her almost "dead white" lifeless face. And, in her side windows reflection, I realized that I had a similar look of fright simultaneously on my own helmeted face. Then THE hit...! NO! At that instant I crashed right into her driver's door, with the front of my motorcycle. Meanwhile I found myself staring at the huge (door mounted) chrome mirror coming right at my throat.

I started my acrobatic flying "routine" all over again, but this time I didn't go dead or even unconscious, like my first aileron gyrations repeated themselves. Let me now give you the details.

Granted I did NOT have much joy for this "corner," or big intersection, anyway. But it did leave a lot to be desired, in my mind and life, since my sudden "literally, impactful" death experience there, had given me, just a few short 6 years earlier. It sure soured my feelings of driving, especially while being right at "my fateful" cross-way. But non-the-less it was about my only route home from work. Not really giving any thought of my earlier horrendous incident, I was just passing through; again, like I had hundreds of times before.

I will admit that my "cautious apprehension" for this busy intersection, had started to somewhat wane. Never imagining that 6 years ago, might have just been a rehearsal for tonight?

I simply thought that it would be a nice quiet enjoyable ride home, on my sweet 1986 Kawasaki Concurs, sport-touring motorcycle. It is something which I so cherish doing; despite the cool spring. And besides, it was a really "fresh" & clear 6:00 pm on a very unusually warm 15th (Ides of March) evening. There was little or No traffic going either direction, in all four lanes except for me cruising along on my cycle, lovin' the ride rather slowly {about 40mph} pulling up to "my" famous, big and usually busy intersection, whose light had just turned green for me to continue through to home.

Now, I queried to myself; was I all alone, or did I have some sort of quiet unseen, companion? No motion. No sound. No touch. Just something eerie; "out there.

As I got closer to the intersection; I saw a white car pull up from my right. I suspected the driver was stopped at their red light, which they he had. But just to be sure, I flashed my high-low 9beam, headlight, hopefully just to make the driver aware of my crossing his car in the interchange.

I passed the old white Buick, which waiting for their green light, enabling them to proceed on. The light had just changed for me so I knew that I had plenty of time to continue going straight ahead. Just as I'm passing that white car, to my right, all I could do other than scream to myself was to verbally erupt with an…"Oh NO!" I immediately saw DEATH, facing me down… one more time! I was instantly staring at a nineteen-ninety's vintage G.M. driver's side door and mirror, it was coming right for me (or else I was coming right for it) and for sure, the "whole thing"… was not going to be a pretty sight. {To say the least}

This is absolutely "Unbelievable!" Just too bizarre! Totally "unreal." A crazy- "coincidental," mindboggling, truly unfathomable event, that is too unimaginable to be real; but still it IS!

"How can this even be?" Any conscious person would agree; that "it just can't be true – it's just too bizarre, for anything like this to actually even happen. Just watch (twice-in the same place, at the same time, in the same direction, at the same intersection, obviously the same cross road, on the same bike, by the same driver, as well as, called in (six years later) by the same employee, then three of the five same police officers, even at the Same time. All duplicating their actions once-again.

Anyone reading this book, would have to say as well, that this just can't be real! Who {on earth} could even get this arranged (6 years later)? I can hear some of you saying to yourselves right now this has to be "made up". It just couldn't all happen exactly like that again, in such an open environment, spaced that far apart. *But it did happen just like that!* and it's all in the police files from two different adjoining departments.

To see how exact all of this is. Please read this next segment that I am putting here. And after reading it, please take note where it comes from; then you'll clearly see why I am saying all of this repetitive "stuff" OK? Thanks. You will end up rather bewildered to say the least.

"The DOA Who Made IT!"

"HUMAN CANNONBALL?... Mythical Flying Super Hero?... Crazy Stuntman?...What is going on here?

Those were some of the questions that must have been surely going through the minds of the many motorists now gridlocked, at a very large and busy highway intersection, at 6:02 in the afternoon, on a hot and sunny, summer Tuesday {July 1st.} just outside Milwaukee, WI."

That Tuesday, which I unmistakably remember, had been a slightly less hectic day than usual, allowed us to close right at 6:00, on the dot. I walked to the front of the store with the other employees, and locked the front door, hopped on my brand new model, "dealer demo", it was a whole new type of Kawasaki. Called the Concours, ZG1000/A1, a "sport-touring" style bike. Of course that 4 cylinder liquid cooled enginer fired right up. I then turned and waved goodbye to all the employees, and got right on that big 4 lane highway, and headed north for home. Just one mile north, there is a very large/busy intersection, that has a high use- on/off ramp from I-94 just to its east about a half mile, and it is a normally active road anyhow, especially when it is a weekday afternoon, and so many people are coming from the city to the suburbs to get home, or where-ever their lives needed to go.

The road to "perdition"?

I had taken this road straight home for over thirteen years now, so you could easily assume, I was quite familiar with all the surroundings; to say the least. So, I apparently was in the left hand lane, my bookkeeping gal Kara, a cute little brunette, who was in the right hand lane now next to me. My cousin Ruth was our receptionist at that time, and she was a pretty long haired brunette too with a super smile, cheerful looks and great demeanor. Those two gals presence sure helped to get the guys attention, and head for the office to buy "that" bike. (Hey common, that's business, marketing, OK?) Besides everything else, they were a couple of real sharp gals, with all of the paper work, and government forms, and the cycle cloths and accessories as well. One of the younger single guys who went to our church needed a job, so I had him working for us; setting up motorcycles out of the crates. His own bike that he was riding home on, had just turned to the left into a raised curb median left turn lane. His back was now away from Kara and I, who were going straight ahead.

Many of the witnesses said, that I must have looked in my mirror and saw another motorcycle pulling up in my lane behind me, so as I'm slowing way down, and coming to the now red light, I veered to the left even further, to give him room in that lane with me. Yes, it is legal to have two motorcycles share a lane, under Wisconsin law. So we just sat their idling our bikes while we waited for the red light to turn green, we were both the first ones in that lane. It was a pretty long light with the left turn indicators switching on ahead of the straight on lanes.

"BAMM! CRASH!" (sorry, no sound effects)There was No screeching of tires from braking sounds at all, or alerting sounds of any sort. Normal traffic noise were all anyone heard. The wallop and crunching sound at the instant impact, extremely startled the biker next to me as he immediately looked down and to his left where he heard the noise. He turned just to see his left leg almost get sheared off by the right front fender of the colliding car, and he saw that I was no longer where I had been sitting, but now my motorcycle was protruding into the front end of this old standard four door sedan, that kept speeding by him, right into the center of all the lanes. The "instantaneous" crash, gave absolutely No one any warning to anyone. "Thanks God", none of the cross traffic got struck by this vehicular concoction. The initial impact was over in just a few seconds.

In that split second, I was struck, by a car that was going at such a high rate of speed; (as the witnesses and police said) that it was almost fifty miles an hour. He obviously had no intention of slowing down or braking, when he hit me. And then sent the motorcycle right into the red lights of that intersection and all of that cross traffic. That old four door sedan that had just hit me at that "deadly" speed, sent me flying upward through the air. "Three stories" (come on) high, (if one can believe thirty-three different witnesses, that are all part of the police reports). And I didn't even have a cape on! (bummer)

As I've said I'm a smaller, not tall "slightly overweight" guy five feet six and a half inches" (pre-accident) 200 + lbs. whose wife is "one incredible cook, and better yet, a spectacular dessert maker. I'm sure she married me just to be her "taste tester," OK, we'll leave that right there. But that "aerial score" that I performed must have been quite a bizarre sight to see). Like I have said earlier. On the way down I proceeded to make two reverse summers-saults, (get jealous high-divers). I landed on the roof of the car that had just crashed into me, and then I caved in that roof right over the driver's head with my feet. But then, they said that I bounced way up and landed on the car roof with my feet again, a second time, but then my feet flew forward, and I hit the roof with my rump, and I bounced and landed on that spot, one more time. (Back breaking land? You'll love this part later; believe me). It must have felt like being on a teeter-totter (when they were still allowed to be in parks and play grounds) if the person on the other end jumps or falls off at the bottom, leaving you to come smashing to earth on the tee-ter-totter board (great pain- could lead to a say "broken back?")

Come fly with me

I proceeded to slide down the front of driver side windshield, and then I actually flew with my full face" helmeted" head draped

81

to the left, (standing up, not horizontal like superman-darn). One of the several policemen from the two adjoining municipalities (they all knew me instantly, when they were "on lunch" or break they would kind-a-like to hang out at the "big" toy store too) took a tape measure in hand, said that I had flown 99 feet, while the other department's officer made his report at 98.75'. I couldn't even get a "lousy 100" feet, maybe for frequent flier mileage, NO? Boy they couldn't even make it 100 feet. Oh well that's" life-NO wait; that's Death!

But you do have to admit to yourself, that flying close to 100 feet through the air, with no landing net, just pavement, couldn't have been a very enjoyable experience, for any one. I hope I was "out" by then. Please let me tell you; that part wasn't fun. Again remember "so I'm told".

As I am quite sure, that you realized, that was from my first book "The DOA Who Made It" written over two years ago. And just as provable of story as this narrative is. Here is a short summary, for you to mull over, as well.

Is the Past *Now* finally GONE for sure?

"Deja' vu" Anyone?

1. Location: 27th. St. (US 41)
2. Direction: due North
3. Crossing: 27th & Rawson ave.
4. Time: 6:02 pm
5. Vehicle: 1986 Kawasaki Concours
6. Drive: Dave Miles
7. 911 caller: Same as 6 years earlier

8. Police: The Same 3 as 6 years earlier
9. Gas station attendant: Same guy working in the gas station (again)

Should, we NOW Say "Oh What a *Coincidence!*" or It must have been his *"Destiny."* Please.

Being that, there absolutely two different city police department reports. And a huge trauma hospital records (both from the same hospital), to prove the validity over and over again.

By now; you're very skeptical or very intrigued. Understood! So what can you do to digest this information; plausibly, that is. No joking around, no dismissal, can't disregard it as say "tomfoolery" either.

Here Are The Facts of Life…, or Death

Please…Isn't twice, enough?

Having traveled by car, rail, air, and ship, even para-sailing and there was Never so much as a scratch received by any of us.

But three miles from my home, going along a multi-lane straight flat dry highway, and to be literally killed, (and or) almost TWICE! It simply can't BE. Can It? Yes! Really! No Joke!

When you read this story, you Will for sure NOT believe in coincidence. If you are a "doubter", just wait. These odds are so incredibly unimaginableable, you'll not think their true. But YES they are true. The same two police department reports verify all of it.

I have never deemed myself as any kind of "daredevil", a "daring" kind of person. So let's ask ourselves; "why is this guy always doing theses acrobatic maneuvers (stunt)? Is he some kind of "showoff", or "attention getter"? NO... I'm NOT!

As I tried to bring forth in "The DOA Who Made It", I just wanted to live a nice "quiet life", living my life with my wife and kids, and doing what I loved best. Selling adult toys...NO don't put your mind there. I mean 1. Motorcycle 2. ATV/UTVs 3. Snowmobiles 4. Jet Skis and the like, power-sports. Yes that kind of adult toy.

Learning to be a preacher and a minister, sure wasn't anything that I had hopes or dreams of, but it sure did take me deep into the Bible and Luther Catechism. Plus, I had to learn about all of the great composers, and all of the weird conditions that they found themselves in, over in Europe, with the various dignitaries, and their bizarre emotional life encounters.

(Ya-No, really they all were a little "loose around the edges") But working through all that, I learned Latin and Classical German – eeuwh.

Here now is an interesting question that I'll ask YOU! I'm sure that most of my readers (like yourself) have heard of Brahms, Bach, Beethoven, Mozart and others from back in the musical renaissance period, NO?

Wolfgang Amadeus Mozart, after composing so many great pieces in his professional career, but he only lived to be 35 years old. This now famous composer died in 757.But...

Do YOU know what he is doing Now?... (DECOMPOSNG) silly.

As a junior in high-school, a single man in his mid-forties; gave me a big challenge. Approaching me, one day in my beginning weeks as a third year high-schooler, he said to me with a big fat thick index finger in my nose. "You get straight B's or better this year, and I will get you a brand new Honda 50!"

In 1966, you couldn't have offered a then 15 year old boy anything greater. "WOW" was my only response. My parents, having been unaware of this till just then, were naturally apprehensive. Not so much that I couldn't get straight B's, but that I should have such a "radical" vehicle. Remember it was 1966, beatnik were still with us and "flower" children were just on the rise, everywhere in the civilized world. (Maybe that's what my parents were really afraid of? Hmmm)

Having described in my last book "The DOA Who Made It," I unknowingly got the world's greatest {C} grade and that changed all of the events of my life. None of us are really proud to get a {C}, but some students just might be glad they at least got one. Non-the-less my {C}, couldn't have been more of an honorary treat, next to all my other {B} grades. No…I'm not kidding. Sure I sacrificed getting a Honda 50, but then you'll see why that was such a blessing. I have tried to get all readers to recognize the principle of {Providence}. Sure, many people simply say "oh- it just so happens", or "what a coincidence".

Those thoughts and comments (if that is you're reasoning) will soon be recognized as completely inadequate, for a genuine & sincere answer. Like I confessed earlier that with a shear lack of a better "socially acceptable" answer I was committed to titling this book just the way it is…."The Doppelganger Did It!"

Having NO real interest in motorbikes, power-scooters, or any form of 2 wheeled transportation, one would think "what has got him so excited then? Did it keep him out of a harder school that he didn't have any desire to go to? "Nope, None of the above" It will be one of the strangest.

Can you say "Let The Good Times Roll?" Maybe even hum the tune that many of us grew up hearing during radio and TV commercials. For at my debilitating {C} almost no one in America could even pronounce, KAWASAKI! Yes, the "motorcycle company" from Japan, that used that tune in so much media and it was as fun to sing as "Have a COKE."

Ten Wheels of Horror

When POLARIS is more than a bright Star

Now, let's move on to the time period between my infamous little feats. Now about say roughly three years after my "Biggy" (the DOA Who Mae It-incident), I was back to work at Oak Creek MotorSports, doing what I loved best (selling motorcycles, and such). Pus my two sons were getting bigger, so they could come "hang-out" with dad at work too. Life was as wonderful as it could get; {so I thought} when right in our parking lot on a hot summers afternoon, I got another taste of "the real-life."

It was just another "GREAT" day at work, selling motorcycles, Jet Ski's, A T V's, and some garden equipment. Or so I thought (again). At the end of each work day we would bring in all of the vehicles that I had put outside, so as to garner some attention, by drive-byes.

I had returned most all of the 8-10 different items, back into the warehouse. I came walking up through some of the short-cut back doors, that were attached to the warehouse and when I got to the front lot, I started up a brand new Polaris six wheel little bump box style utility ATV.

As I got on and grabbed the handlebars, I turned it to go across in front of the showroom and then to the back, to our attached warehouse. All of this was paved and open all the way to the back lot.

I accelerate quite nicely, and it's just a parking lot, so I made a wider curve, and much to my horror, was a big older Chevy truck just "flying" down the driveway, heading for the main highway but still real fast while so close to the driveway entrance. The driver was sort of coming to the road rather diagonally. He was exiting toward the corner of our building, for no rational reason at all, as well as going at quite a high speed already.

As "fate" would have it, I was just starting to turn right, with this rather big six wheel dump-truck ATV. For whatever reason, I don't know, I suddenly looked up to see this truck aiming right for me.

When I saw that I was going to get hit; all I could remember was what some cyclist had told me years earlier, which was, "If you get hit by a car on the front end just do everything in your power to Not slide up the hood, because the edges of the windshield wipers will slice you apart like sharp knives." That fear has always stuck with me, and now I am finding myself sliding up over and across the hood of that full size pickup, aiming right for the windshield and of course the wipers just in front of them. Staring at those lancets, just waiting to slice the whole front of my body.

I can honestly say that I reacted to that sight, and somehow tried to get to the "other side of the truck instead of straight up the front. All I could remember at that point was my foot getting almost trapped under the wiper blade mounts. Thankfully I did a roll and tumble on the asphalt and laid there till some employees came running over. Just another day in paradise, so it seemed. But this time things were different. Well sort of anyhow.

The "quickie", I referenced at the beginning of this chapter, wasn't any more than my breviloquent (short period of time) stay at St. Lou's hospital. So…"It doesn't count!" I was taken by ambulance and picked up by my wife, in under 3 hours. And I was only in the emergency room.

That astronomical word is known and found in some dictionaries but not all of them.

My point behind telling you about language and words; they are all "man-made" and the only reason that one you might make up or me, is that fact that nobody knows what it might mean. That is really all there is to it.   {Sorry English grammar teachers}. Remember this; the one rule about the English language grammar is that "there really are NO rules."

Chapter Five

Can You DIG IT?

Early the next morning they took me to a regular room, where I had another experience that I can NEVER imagine having to tolerate again.

Just laying on that medical crib full of hoses and wires, I was suddenly approached by a very senior doctor. He was sort of slumped over in a rather "osteoporosis" type bow. With his entry, it was quite obvious that he would be in "command" of the room. With him came three "interns" two male and one female". They were in their twenties, while the older doctor was well into his mid to late sixties.

He proceeded to step around the bottom end of the bed. He then came over to my right {window side}. I now noticed that he too was carrying something, being now within my view, I noticed that it was one of those large "moonshine" type wine bottles, with a finger hole at the top. He set it down right next to the bed and window. Erecting himself; he leaned over and then reached over towards my right shoulder and then pulled the hospital gown down a ways, to expose the upper right side of my chest.

BAD to the bone

With his two aged partially "hooked" middle fingers he began feeling and tapping my chest, until he stopped and pressed down; which really hurt. He then nodded and retracted a long metal wide fountain pen looking device, from his medical coat pocket.

With a little bandage looking piece of gauze he rubbed the area, and immediately set the lower tip of this device onto my skin; where he thought it should be placed. Then holding the six or seven inch long apparatus between his two palms. Not waiting very long, he spun the ink pen looking tool back and forth between his 2 hands causing the little piece of equipment to act just like a mini-oil well drill.

Please let me tell you (oxygen mask or not) I screamed! So loud the three interns were ready to jump into each other's laps. Either he didn't use ANY or he just didn't wait long enough for the local anesthetic to work, but that digging tool tore up a lot of my skin in a downward motion.

After ten or fifteen seconds of "drilling", he stopped and looked up and said "DAMM"; hit a rib. So he then took one, index finger and with an encumbrance of smooth pressure felt around my upper chest/shoulder area again, and moved the despicable tool over his little pencil mark and dug in again. My arms were restrained with Velcro on the bed sides and of course I had the oxygen mask covering my nose and mouth or else he would not have been able to do that "well drilling" activity again.

With the intensity of the first "experiment" he rapidly spun that protrusion stick back and forth, while holding downward pressure on it yet another time. The real interesting part of this episode, was that he forgot to put any pain remover in that location. So you can simply imagine that extra pain that I tried to withstand. Oh Man! Did that hurt....BAD!

This is one experience I wouldn't wish on anybody; especially going along with the rest of my body's pain, which was permeating all parts of my immobile carcass, right now.

As the tutoring doctor kept spinning that protrusion, it seemed like it was never going to stop. The pain just kept getting more intense by the stroke. Suddenly the three interns standing directly behind and to the back of the doctor heard what I lurched at; the ripping and tearing of flesh, as the epidermis eradicator punctured all of my skin and muscles in that spot. I let out with a muffled scream and jerked my head away.

Obviously, he wasn't done yet, because after his look of delight on his face meant something pleasing to him, he pushed down even much harder, without so much as a "once around" spiral. And then we all heard the rip, as it punctured my desolate of oxygen right lung. My murmured scream was even realized by the patient in the adjacent bed.

Again, with a look of joy; the doctor who was so proud of his display to the other three that he felt satisfied by removing the "micro-assiduous staff, out of my chest.

Alas! It must be {all over}, right? WRONG! This abecedarian then reached into his deeply large medical jacket and pulled out a fifteen to eighteen inch plastic pipe, and then struggled to insert it into that faintly bleeding and burning chamber he just dug into my bosom.

Twisting and turning sporadically while exerting vigorous pressure, he kept lowering it farther and farther down towards the lower center of my abdomen. Finally, he ceased this aggressive intrusion and stood upright to admire his work.

Then bending down to the floor, he straightened up again holding large glass brown jug with a finger hole in it and perpetuated his tasks, by stuffing a cork like object into the top, that had two or three nozzles protruding upward. After that was in place he attached a hose on either orifice or the other end to an electric pump mechanism, then he held the hard plastic tub, which was now three fourths in me and slid the pinching tight end of the hose onto it. It then made an eerie sound and gurgle, which as we could see through the transparent hose, was pulling up and out bloody water.

The thought of "What did I do to deserve all this?" Kept haunting me. Nonetheless. "How long will I have this thing hooked up?" I queried the doctor, as he turned and started to exit this medical enclosure. It should be in for at least a few days. Oh, I bemoaned.

How are you going to then re-inflate my lung? I asked. He said it will do it all by itself, once all of the fluid is removed. "Really." I quipped. Then they all walked out, leaving me to my salubrious undertaking.

Within an hour or so, another doctor came into my room then up to my bed, thankfully all alone. He very quickly pulled out his stethoscope, and began listening all over my chest and abdominal cavity. I questioned "what are you looking for- doctor?" He replied "We have reason to believe that your pancreas may have gotten punctured, or shut down." "Oh!" I hesitantly burped. "So now what?" I then fearfully asked. "Well…we'll keep an eye on it for a while and see what we find." Came the return comment.

He then coiled up the stethoscope's hoses and quietly tip-toed out; like he was leaving a funeral visitation, or something.

I spent the next two days listening to that disgusting vacuum pump sucking the fluids out of my body, but I did notice that this aqueous solution, seemed to be "lightening up a bit. None the less; having a pliable duct protruding from your chest is a ghoulishly uncomfortable sight.

Not like my first tarriance to St Lou's hospital (which lasted a month), I never got so much as a visit from my parents; in as much as they were over in Ireland before I got it the second "anathematic" time, and were completely unaware of my second "encounter."

Musing over this; I became committed on getting out of this hospital before my parent's returned home from their vacation in Ireland. And that means that I won't be in there for more than ten days, total. I quietly and complacently mentioned to my wife that I could be leaving in a few days; after being in that bed now for seven full days. Yes, she did balk, thinking that I would be in there for at least another week. "They might even let me go by Wednesday, they just want to wait and see a little longer." I interjected; and let me go by this Sunday.

Finally, when Tuesday came around, the serious older nurse took my blood pressure and checked my heart rate as well. Then I commented to her that I was expecting to leave on Wednesday. She abruptly broke in to my words by saying the most ultimate thing every man wants to hear a woman say. "You aren't leaving here until I hear you pass gas." Really did she just say that? Yes those were her words. I smiled and said that's the "nicest thing" any woman has ever said to me. I also told her that I thought I was doing fine. She snapped back with "I've got to know all those organs are working right down there."

The woman that I perceived was the head nurse on that floor had never so much as ever said a word to me prior. She entered my room on Monday; now after five days of my medical incarceration, and took the oxygen mask off of me, and removed all of the hoses and pumps.

When the doctor finally came in, I insisted to him that I had to be "out" of there by Wednesday at noon. Teetering back on his heels, he said "Well See." "No" I commanded in an authoritative manner. I can lay around and heal up at home. "Now that the oxygen is removed and my lung has re-inflated, it's important for me to go."

"Ok... I guess", he rather sheepishly whimpered back. "But we're going to have to just make sure, that everything is alright." "Yes sir." I clapped back quickly.

So...Mom & Dad, How was Ireland?

Who do I think I am? Telling the doctors what to do, or when to do it? I know that I have no right to boss them around, but let's blame it on that left-handed only child, little brat syndrome. We good? Hope so, anyhow.

So the tenth day came and my wife got there about 11 am, and I took my bag of a few items, like a breathing tool, that I had to blow in 10 or 12 times twice a day. I, once again "hopped" into the wheelchair and she pushed me to the elevators. We were getting good at this, by now

Instead of going home, we went straight to the Milwaukee airport, which was only about five miles away. Unlike us ever having done this before, we pulled up to the passenger pick-up area, my parents were waiting for us, with their suitcases and "weird" scowls on each of their faces. We opened the trunk and my dad put the luggage in and came around and opened the back door, so he and my mom could get in.

SURPRISE! It's me...Again

Now, here I am, sitting in the passenger side of my parent's car, in hospital garb, and a light robe. Turning the window down, I smiled and said "Hi, how was your trip?" And all my dad said "NOW! What's going on here with you two?" What? I shrugged my shoulders in disbelief. Why is Elsbeth driving and your dressed in your "jammies?"

"Well....we had a little situation the day after you left for Ireland." I humbly and quietly replied. "What do you mean?" came from the back seat. Oh, I just found out that little old ladies from South Milwaukee don't like me." "What are you talking about, now?" my mom chimed in

"You see, I was coming home, like always and got up to 27th and Rawson again....You know my famous/infamous intersection. I wasn't speeding or anything when the light turned green for me, back by the Rafters restaurant; and so I went through and just after I past a car headed west, I smacked right into the driver's door of an Old's 98, that a woman who had just turned her car to the right so bad, that she suddenly decided to do a "cross-body block," left hand correction, right in front of me. I could hear my mom's frighteningly tearful and gasping moan. My dad just grunted with "you gonna be alright?" "Ya well as best as can be expected." I sorta chirped

"So what were my options Dad? Like you know I do, I started flying again (Ha Ha). I crushed my chest against the handlebars and fairing, then I went up. But dad, I went flying upward for so long, that it seemed like time just stopped. I started talking to myself and to God, saying. "Well here I come again, hope you're ready for me this time." Crash WHAM! I hit what, hood, roof, road; I didn't have any idea, because it was so dark outside. Believe it or not Dad, I bounced again; so I said to God "caught you by surprise; huh?" ha ha ha, then I hit something again, hood, roof, road, trunk who knows? "Beats me, whatever I hit, the next time. But just once more I went up and came down all the way over into the median."

After a hard thump, I felt myself laying face upward, right in the middle of the 4 lane highway, on the median which means that I must have flown quite a ways from the far right lane to land in the middle of the boulevard.

But I have to tell you that I really thought that I was just lying there watching myself die. My mother tearfully grimaced, when she heard me then say. "Because I couldn't breathe, just a slight gasp and *Nothing*... no intake of oxygen. Or even exhale, for that matter. I did lay there staring at all the stars, while wondering how soon I might be going up there too."

After what seemed like an eternity , a couple of people came running over to me, just trying to get me to "hang on" that some-body had already dialed 911 and the cops should be there soon. Yah; but "soon enough? Was my query. My thoughts were ...."ya right." I wasn't able to bring any air in. But before I knew it, a few police started running over to me with an oxygen mask in hand. They put it over my nose and mouth. The elastic strap snapped on the back of my head. While doing those projects they looked a little closer and blurted out "Dave...Dave Miles, Hey man this is your corner isn't it?" I groaned inaudibly, "Please guys no funnies right now please."

Nothing else happened for what I thought was an extended amount of time, till I heard the rescue squad pull up and the back doors fling open, and two EMT's jumped out, with a stretcher in tow.

"Now I was awake for this whole thing, dad, but what really got me gruffed, was when they all started arguing about which hospital to take me to." Under the oxygen mask I kept trying to say "Lou's, Lou's." Figuring that they really did help keep me alive the last time. As I say in "The DOA Who Made It" I sure am glad that I didn't sue them, because they all suddenly agreed to take me to St. Lou's hospital instead of the other medical center, down in South Milwaukee, which I must confess, that I never heard of any-body who went in to that place as a patient came out as anything but a corpse. I know that's not true...but.

My mom queried "David, shouldn't you still be in the hospital?" "Ya mom, I certainly could be, but I wanted to be with El. when we picked you up at the airport." Let's drive back over to the hospital and get you back in." My dad snapped back quickly saying.

"NO! NO!" I yammered back. I'm just fine, I'll keep healing at home really dad really." There is nothing more that they can do for me there anyway. I'd just be laying there healing up. Really, I can do that from home. My mom and dad both {groused} at it, but Elsbeth kept drive towards our house.

When we arrived to our home, we all got out, and at my parents continued insistence to return to the hospital; I found myself with a walker, rushing (ya right) to the front door. For some strange reason, I don't have "nice feelings" about being in any hospital as a patient. Really? Ya think? Wonder why...hmm?

Once I finally got in the house and to a chair, then urging them to go home, I felt much better in my own surrounding's. However I felt a lot of pain; all around my chest, and even my legs and shoulders. Then I laid around the house for a few more months. So I could practice with my little breathing device which let me keep breathing and expand my lung capacity.

So here I go back into the "healing" mode...again. Just sitting around the house, was killing me, too. No...come on; must know that wasn't literal. (Good ole English language, again0

Chapter Six

Pain has NO home...
It goes anywhere "it" wants

The rest of that spring and summer went by rather uneventful. "Whew", is all I can say about that. After I got back to work, it was a great time selling cycles and Jet Ski's again; and reminiscing with my old customer-friends, and we sure chatted, all about the last accident.

But then, of course the word had spread to Kawasaki corporate, and when we got to the dealer show that fall, I only had about a month or so of healing. I had a "latta splanin ta do ("Sicilian mobster quote?); to all the corporate "big shots" and the so many dealer friends that I had acquired around the country.

END of AN ERA....

Going along now for about the next two years things were pretty much back to "normal," whatever in the world normal was supposed to mean in my life. Then one day...here it comes.

Very quietly, a man who owned another motorcycle shop, that had moved to within a mile of us and built and built big new facility for his Honda franchise about a year and a half earlier; came to Hank, (who I talked a lot about in the first book) who was the owner & total stock holder of our company. He presented a request that because we were "eating their lunch" in sales, and that they just couldn't compete with our clientele base that we had built up for that almost 30 years; wondered if we would be interested in "buying them out?" Taken by surprise at the offer, we just responded that we would have to think about it.

We really didn't know that they were NOT selling a lot of their Honda product, but with that big new facility also came huge costs to contend with. And they needed a lot more volume just to compensate for their heavy load of expenses.

After talking with the accountant and our lawyer, we were going to offer to sell them our franchise's (Kawasaki, BMW, Suzuki, Arctic Cat, Polaris, Evinrude, and Suzuki outboards. We were sure that they couldn't afford it, but we thought hey let's see.

Well that got them to thinking, but when they came back a few weeks later, they were willing to talk with us about such a thing.

Now, here is where the real "glitch" came in. Twenty five years earlier, Hank, our old family friend, and now my boss for thirty years, as well; had the attorneys' create a purchase agreement, lease agreement, a will, and take out an insurance policy for a huge amount, so that in the death of Hank, the life insurance policy would pay for the inventory and tools, so I could keep Oak Creek MotorSports inc going. That was all well and good; just one problem. Hank didn't die, and yet he now wanted to sell, but the agreement demanded that as long as I am employed at Oak Creek MotorSports, it had to be sold to me (first).

There was one small problem, with this whole scenario. I didn't have anywhere near enough money to now buy out Hank's total stock in the company. Somewhere between one and two million dollars, that is. So, with Hank not being dead the insurance money wouldn't be available to pay for the business. Sure, I could have "squeezed every friend and relative that I knew, then turn my house over to the bank for collateral, plus everything else that I owned; and then {maybe} squeezed out almost enough, but probably still not even then.

Another portion of mine & my wife's life that I haven't revealed yet; is that in 1988, the two of us went through a class from an organization based in Georgia, called "Crown Financial Ministries". It is a wonderful "para-church confederation", that teaches something that almost NO ONE can imaging, which is almost inconceivable to most people today.

I will start by asking YOU, if you might know what the {five] most often talked about subjects are in the Bible? Ok you guessed that first one:

1. Love
2. Faith
3. Patience
4. Humility
5. MONEY! What? "Money…You say?" Yup, there it is. Really "No Kidding"

Just think about it, for a minute. What is the "one thing" that touches every human being equally, usually with force and prominence? It doesn't matter what name you put on it. (Ruble, Yen, Pound, Euro, or Dollar). They ALL work the same. What better way could God get His point across to we humans?

Many Anglo-Saxons (maybe everybody) have heard the phrase "money is the root of all evil." When in fact, that is a terrible misquote from the New Testament book of I Timothy 6:10, which actually Says "for the {love} of money is the root of all evil." Ready for a shocker? God has absolutely *Nothing* against having wealth. Moses, Abraham, Samson, Job, King David, King Solomon, were Old Testament {saints} who were quite well to do.

The problem isn't with money, but rather in the control that those who possess it, often get caught under. The real culprit is GREED! We humans are so weak in our self-worth that we feel we need more "control" of whatever! Money gives us {clout, power, influence and control}, which we think will make us feel better; when we all have heard of how the lottery winner blows it all and becomes totally devastated when it is gone. Sports figures and very well off actors, are all susceptible. Which just shows us that it is something else we can't control.

Yes! I am one of those who claims to be a firm believer in God and the Bible. That being the case, I resolved many years ago, back in my Concordia high school days, that if God has something to say; and I believe that He has created and sustains everything, that it probably would be pretty smart on my part, to listen to what He has to say. So, if He has a lot to teach us about money, maybe this is a good place to pay attention.

The Bible NEVER says or implies that it is wrong to borrow money; only that there are a few prerequisites that should be dealt with first.

Now, you see why borrowing one or two million dollars (if it were possible) wouldn't be a very smart thing for me to do. So I had to let that option go. Plus a business owner needs to have an account of "cash" just to pay bills. Our family friend and later my boss Hank Hoffmann, would keep reminding me that" It takes money to MAKE money."

We all know people who are basic hypocrites (say one thing, but do another). Like so many folks that ride their Hardley's cause it's American; while driving their BME, Mercedees, Toyota, Lexus, Nissan, or Infinity cars and SUV's. Between my upbringing and my ministerial training at Concordia high/college, I found that God really doesn't want that, from any kind of spiritual leader. We all know that their "credibility" sure collapses when others find out how "phony that is. (Sell Chevy's / drive Ford). Weekly people would come to me for help with their finances. I have been a volunteer financial counselor since 1988. For me to tell someone, who is desperately attempting to right their "financial ship", by me saying that they must learn to budget, and get out of debt; just wouldn't be honest for me to say while be so extremely in debt myself.

So after I was threatened to be fired or quit, I thought my days selling Kawasaki's might be all over. But a few months later I found out that wasn't true, either. Here is where some more exciting adventures came for me again.

She-boy-again

A good friend and fellow Kawasaki & Hmm hmm Hardley dealer, about sixty miles north of Milwaukee, in a small city on

Lake Michigan, called Sheboygan, questioned me if I would be interested in coming up to Sheboygan, to sell Kawasaki's for him. He told me that I wouldn't be subject to having to sell those "other" bikes. So after a little thought, I said sure, and started driving an hour north {to do my thing}, sell Kawasaki's again.

The drive, going through downtown Milwaukee twice a day, wasn't usually all that bad, but it still was a long drive. Yet worth it, I thought, to do what I loved. Which we all know by now, must be selling Kawasaki's.

The best part of the job was riding one of my Kawasaki's to work every day for an hour at a time. The folks that worked up there new of my collection and seemed to want to see every cycle that I had. So periodically I would bring up a different bike to show off.

One nice rather warm spring day, I finally decided to bring up my ultimate "crotch rocket" which happened to be a 1985 Kawasaki GPZ 750 turbo. In its "hey-day" it could loudly proclaim to be the "world's fastest stock production vehicle." Please let me tell you that IT WAS! Whew that thing could scream.

The morning that I had decided to take a long ride up there, I got through the city, then kept going straight up the [I-43] system due north for about 35 more miles, it then curved to the right headed towards a small city in southeast Wisconsin, known as Port Washington. Which was only about a mile and a half east. Then, while passing by on the north side of the small city, the express way curved back to straight north again. From there it was about another twenty miles or so to Sheboygan, Wisconsin.

There really wasn't much traffic then at about nine fifteen or so, so I just stayed sort of hunched over the gas tank and kept cruising. Ok, the speed limit up there out in the rural part of the eastern side of the state, close to Lake Michigan, is/was sixty-five miles per hour.

Coming near the off-ramp to Port Washington and then sweeping to the north, there was a high overpass bridge with on/off ramps on both sides. Now I had seen many times how a Wisconsin State Patrol squad car would sit on the high side just a little off the on-ramp lane going north. So if or let's say when a speeder would be passing under that over-pass bride and anticipating the ninety degree turn north the radar on the squad car would go off, and they would just keep going down the grade, get on the [I] system, and with a mile or so pull the speeder over and issue them a "hefty" speeding ticket.

All of that now being said, I was just passing under the bridge, and easing my GPZ 750 Turbo into that nice wide path curve to the north. As I was winding around that contour, I (of course) pulled back on the handlebar throttle, and made that straight-away look slow.

Having not paid attention to the possible radar trap or my speedometer; I just kept screaming along, pretty much uncontested by other vehicles. About three to four miles further up I-43, I finally realized that although my shoulders {which were about the only thing that could be seen by a turbo driver, in the mirror, I had some company. Yes bright red lights flashing away and a loud siren, that I could finally hear, the closer it approached, was rapidly accelerating right behind me. Not being foolish enough to hope that the State Patrol squad, was going to some {other} event; I started to slow and work my way off the traveling lane to let them go by. A-HUH. No such luck. It was braking right behind me. Darn!

Once we were both stopped, I put my side-stand down, and started to remove my beautiful color-matched red and black Turbo helmet. The Wisconsin State Patrol officer got close to the back of my bike, when they bellowed out, in what almost sounded like female's voice? It really didn't matter; I knew my life was NOW close to over. "Do you know how fast you were going?" Now with my helmet off, I turned to my left and said "No." "YOU Just stay seated-right there!" I chanced it. "Yes Ma'am; Maybe around seventy five-or so?" I squeaked.

Instantly, I received back a loud clear "Ninety Nine miles an hour." These words did come from one of the largest female human beings that I have ever laid eyes on. A face, no scowl, like a bull dog. And the eyes and teeth were aiming right at me. What made her look even more imposing was, that she had her arms spread out and into bone crunching V. Not so much like an eagle, rather a Vulture} as she was firmly depositing, (I thought I heard almost heard a thud) on her cranium, one heavily intimidating "ultra-wide brim" police fedora. Her very "solid" leather boots went up to her knees, and her strut reminded me of documentaries that I have seen about the Nazi SS, back in the late thirties and early forties. This'll hurt more than the accidents, I'll bet. Were my thoughts just then?

"Dead Meat!" Was the only thing that went through my mind after that point. "I know you weren't racing or driving recklessly, because I was following you for over five miles at almost one hundred miles an hour." Came sternly, at me. To say the least though, her tone was certainly not congenial as she kept strutting closer and closer to me.

All I could do was shrug my shoulders, and pray for a quick death. I was absolutely sure that I was on the cusp of total disaster, and would be spending some time in the local jail.

She came up to me and coarsely demanded my driver's license, {which I used to have} as rapidly as I could, I pulled it out of the back-pocket of my blue jeans. Then opening my wallet I removed it, and sheepishly placed it into the tight black leather, human vice-grip hand, that she had slightly protruded, toward me. On her way back to the squad, she turned and said "This is NOT the name on the license plate. So whose bike is this? Stuttering I said it is mine, I just bought it a while ago and rebuilt it; (All true, but the word just should have meant six years ago). I haven't got the title transferred yet. She didn't even slow down on her way back to the squad car, while I was pleadingly yearning to have her understand my plight.

After about, what felt like an eternity, or at least four or five minutes, she once more stepped out of the squad car (which then raised) up and then turning around, she reached in and grabbed her exorbitantly large police hat, again. She then suddenly reached towards her shoulder, then turning her head away from me, she talked to the microphone and began to almost parade towards me and the Kawasaki 750 GPZ Turbo. Which I thought I'd probably never see again. Approaching the back of the motorcycle she had my license in one hand and a receipt pad in the other (whew…not a gun). "Here it comes." I thought. "Good bye world."

"Now look here, I've got to take this emergency call. Whose bike is this and why don't the plates match the motorcycle or you?" Was her query. "Ma'am-Officer" I humbly returned. "I bought the bike years ago, and did what I could to restore it. I ran a Kawasaki dealership down in Oak Creek, then I started working up here in Sheboygan, where they wanted me to show it to them. I'm sorry that I didn't see your lights sooner, but the mirrors don't stick out far enough past my shoulders."

She stared me in the eyes and said, "I'm inclined to believe you, but Buster you better watch out. Here is your license and ticket." Then she handed me my driver's license, and the speeding ticket wrapped around it. I bowed defencively and thanked her and grasped my helmet strap, then swung back around to get on my bike.

She quickly pranced back to her car, and left the flashing red light on and accelerated "pedal to the metal" leaving a streak of exhaust. I whimsically wished her goodbye.

While opening the fold, of the speeding ticket, (I was afraid that my blue jeans were going to start getting wet,) which surrounded my driver's license. I looked down to see the "home equity loan" cost of the ticket, and snatched a view and suddenly realized that it was a "Warning Notice." The total cost was; (get this), really $23.50 and no points. True I am Not Kidding Really! And I definitely know, it wasn't because of my "good looks." You will now know why I looked straight up high, smiled and loudly said "Thank You!"

Somebody {up there} was sure looking out for me, and I definitely knew/know that I didn't deserve it; but strong praise was submitted on my part anyhow. Like so much of everything else in our lives; we are far from perfect. In other words, we're deserving of full castigation.

But "He" does love us so much, that either committing intentional or accidental infirmity's we can realize as forgiven, after we have been brought into his "fold." Notice that I used the word infirmity; which is actually another word for a "type" of Sin. There! I said it! So are you happy now? Let's face it; you knew it was going to come sooner or later, in this type of book; NO?

Actually there are several distinctions to the *types* of sin. 33 different words as such. Here are some of the more well known. Believe it or not God (Jehovah, YHWH or some might even say Allah) will, and does forgive all sorts and types of sins. It's NOT as much as the action, but the heart attitude behind it.

After we were all given "free wills," to live our lives our {own way}, God knew that this wasn't going to work for eternity. Because Now that we have "Sinned" none of us can live forever. So Now What Options are then left for US? Because we all know that none of us are perfect. Certainly NOT Me! You do want to live forever; right? Or just have the 'best time" that you can while on this big ball of dust and water?

Here are a few of the most notable of the 33, yet slightly different words that may be thought to be the "fun" killer known as sin. Pretty much any word that a person knows as less than perfect would count too.

1. Trespass
2. Iniquity
3. Infirmity
4. faults, mis-deed
5. offend
6. Unrighteous
7. Transgress
8. Covet
9. Peccadillo
10. Anger

The Hebrew word simply means *"to MISS"*.

For those of you who don't know...These are NOT the Ten Commandments in the Bible.

And note; Yes the Quran has Ten commandments, and yet even many more.

God Does Want Obedience. But even more, He wants love and to be respected as our Righteous Holy God and our SAVIOR and sustainer!

Okay okay... let's go back to Sheboygan

I'm quite sure that you'll already know this, but I sure didn't do any more speeding the next 20 miles to the cycle shop that I worked at,at least for that day. Problem is, when I got there and pulled into the parking lot, my friend-now boss, looked down at his wrist, and then back up to me. When I shut the bike off, and removed my helmet, he, Bill {my ex-boss/friend?} started to shake his head and motioned down to the 750 GPZ Turbo. Inquisitively he commented in a dismayed sort of look, "The World's fastest production Street vehicle, and today you're late?

"You won't believe what just happened to me!" I forcefully announced. "Oh boy, here it comes," was the one reply, he made. "But Bill please just listen {please–again}," I started to quiver when trying to explain that mornings events. He appeared to almost disbelieve what I was telling him; yet he had a big grin on his faces, anyhow. And after all these years that we knew each other, he knew that I wouldn't lie, but the twenty three dollar "warning ticket" just seemed to make it more implausible.

Walking away in a very (skeptical mood) step, he said. "Just get these bikes out on display." "Whew!!"

Now, I "Gotta" Bone to pick with WHO?

About 4 months later, it was around mid to late August or so, and I was on my great big 6 cylinder Kawasaki Voyager 1300 touring bike. (Some Wisconsin and Minnesota based companies can still only make 2 cylinders. The rest is over their head; I guess). It was a fuel injected six cylinder liquid cooled ultra-high quality touring motorcycle. And it was Very quiet and soo soo smooth, besides. Best way to describe it would be calling it a "Land Yacht." With that being said, all of that luxury did come at a hefty 1000 pounds of weight, {fueled}.

I was so comfortably cruising home that weekday afternoon about a little past five pm. But please remember, it does still stay light out for a long time; say somewhere between eight or eight thirty. That stretch of the "I-43" highway, which was about 10 miles south of Sheboygan itself was usually quiet from traffic that day.

Motorcycle or not, almost anyone could envision the fright at what I am about to share. Maybe a half mile or so in front me, and going my same direction, when I glanced way ahead, I noticed a big open top semi-trailer that was "barreling" down the road ahead of me at a pretty fast clip. The speed limit is 65mph and everyone including trucks are doing at least 75 mph. There was a type of gentle "S" curve, continuing south and I was in the lane next to where the semi was traveling. It didn't dawn on me until I suddenly saw what happened atop the back

111

of the semi-trailer. The trailer had tall aluminum sides on it, and the load was heaping over the sides. There had been a full two lane road bump similar to say like a speed bump in a parking lot. It was paved, but very noticeable. You could always feel it, and it would make a shorter wheel-based vehicle like a cycle really bounce.

In many opportunities of conversation with other bikers through-out the years, we all agreed that there couldn't be a much worse scenario (than maybe a deer jumping out in front of a bikers ride) than what I am about to express, it took place on that beautiful warm sunny August day. I was listening to the radio, (which was part of the bike.) The semi up ahead had just traversed the soft S curve in the right lane. I was in the left lane, coming up behind it, then about three to four car lengths away, the trailer hit that bump which sent the rear-end bouncing and unsure of what just happened, I suddenly looked forward again, to see this huge long raw bone from what I think was a cow leg fall to the paved surface right behind the semi, it bounced with vivacity from behind the semi-trailer over to the other lane which I was coming up on. It swirled and stopped just cross wise shortly before I arrived. Brake slamming wouldn't let me avoid it in any way. I had been doing about sixty five (posted speed), just as I saw it.

The remarks that all of us bikers would agree on, was if something like a big water pipe, or any strong tubular shaped item came to be right ahead of the driver's front wheel, it is almost "certain death" or at least, a very serious destructive calamity. There would be no calibrating what it is going to do when the wheel hits it, and the motorcycle would develop a wild "swailling" (my own *homemade* word) gesture that simply would NOT let the driver have any control of the front wheel, as it would lash back and forth from the left to the right.

Guess What? Sure enough there were no other options for me there either, but hit it and pray, (simultaneously). I should say, that when the front wheel hit the bone; the handlebars instantly shook and jerked me to the left, as I was trying to divert the bike farther to the outside of that lane. I didn't let go of the handlebars but I tried to lock my arms as straight and hard as I could. But as expected the whole thing started to shimmy, almost uncontrollably. All I was able to accomplish was to decelerate the throttle, and keep tension on the bars, while braking slowly so as not to cause the bike to convulse, any more than it already was.

This occurrence was truly the most "frightening" of my life. The big "DOA Who Made It" episode, where I had absolutely NO memory of, and the ATV Truck incident in the parking lot, or even the "cross body blocking" event that the little old lady pulled on me, didn't scare me as much as to think about tipping over on two wheels, especially at that high rate of speed. But this was simply horrifying. It gave me the feeling that the front wheel fell off, with the bobbing, and twisting that was going on. An instant impact that occurs almost never, but still lasts so long, and let a person envision all of the anxious scenarios, that are about to come.

Seconds/minutes later? I could not reckon the time, but I stayed upright. [A quick note that I had learned from dirt-bike riding was to NEVER put your feet down off the pegs; because, when your feet are on the pegs, the center of gravity is pushed so much lower, for better control, otherwise when your feet are off the cycle it moves all of the way up to the sea. I was slowing down, while the front wheel kept shimmying back and forth. Then finally straightening some, as I even gripped tighter. I suddenly thought that I saw the bone spine off the right of me and the bike. Finally I got over on the left hand gravel covered shoulder. Upon finally getting totally stopped and I was able to get the side stand down, I almost slid my {full pants} off the seat, onto the gravelly grass surface.

Never before, have I found myself literally shivering and shaking. And yes I did look down, believing that I must have wet my pants too; but they somehow still looked rather dry. I fell to the ground in a legs cross sort of yoga fashion, and kept crying "Thank You, Thank You, Thank You! Which was the most appropriate thing that a person (like myself) who believes in God and protective angels'; with some benevolence thrown in the mix, was able to utter.

Still, spared of any heart attacks yet; I did have a lot of fun up there in Sheboygan, Wisconsin, even with those hm. Hm. Hardley's surrounding me every day. Hey; it's all in fun, like a Chevy lover, to a Ford lover. Or the guy who loves his RAM, over a Silverado, or F250.

I could Hardley bear it...Oh well!

But all those Hardley's in the same showroom, as the beautiful Kawasaki's. {Water/Oil?} And Yes I did even sell one once. (This is great.) It was around the middle of March and business was still waning, so I got a marketing idea, and called all of the Indian based casinos, that are located in Wisconsin.

We had an all-black and special stripped Hardley "Sturgis" model, which is appropriately named for the small town up in South Dakota. The first full weekend of August every year the town turns into the 5th largest city in America for 4 days. Cyclists from "all over" including overseas come for a super huge bikers rally. And of course the company that purports itself as being "Made in the USA" made a special edition for a year or so just simply named the *Sturgis*.

I tried thinking for the casinos, what a "great idea" for them to use as a "come on" in their advertising and promotion departments. They could have it on display and maybe someone could win it.

So I called five or six casinos, and they all listened but showed little interest. I contacted the one Indian Casino in The Wisconsin Dells area. They seemed somewhat a little interested as well, and just let it go with the classic "just let us think about it." Ok, so I said sure and hung up.

Here comes late June, the same year, and I get a call from the big casino, in the Wisconsin Dells area, they suddenly wanted to talk to me about my suggested ideas, in regards to the Sturgis motorcycle.

Their first question was "Do You Still Have It? And if so How Much would I sell it to them for? I eagerly replied that YES we still own it and would be willing to sell it to them. It was like new and in perfect shape, and they were going to give it away in late summer so the winner could drive "IT" to Sturgis, South Dakota, themselves, and show off.

My knowing the relative rarity of the ten year old bike, and its awesome showroom countenance, I couldn't just give it away

115

to them to use as winning for some gambling achievement. It only had about 10,000 miles on it so I told them that they could have it for 5 grand more than it "stickered for", brand new. "What?" was the surprised return? "Look" I casually said, "You're going to make a whole lot of money on this thing, and you can't use any other bike than a Sturgis." Hmm… Came the grown, "We'll have to think about it and talk it over. If we're still interested, we'll call you." "Okay" I chirped back. "Good Bye" "Secret…" to readers who may happen to be a salesperson as well. "Don't tell your boss, when you are trying to over-charge for something like a collectible, until IT's a sale. They just don't understand. If it doesn't work out "so be it", but if it does, you become the "hero" of the store.

Three days later, I got another call from them and they said that the only way they would purchase that bike was to have me give it to them at a much lower price that they were offering. I just said "NO." OK…ok, but only if it came with "free delivery". "It most *certainly* will be delivered to you for free" I said. "Now just give me the address, that I can send the invoice to, thank You." You should have seen the faces of my friend/boss, and all of the dealer's employees, when they saw that contract. Just like my daddy always said "One Man's trash, is another man's treasure."

My (unexpected) Squeeze

I really don't know if Angel's can be proud of their accomplishments or are most likely supposed to be humble. I am one who (especially now) believes in "Guardian Angels" from the text you just read and in the last book, you've got to see why.

The bible tells us in the New Testament book of Hebrews chapter 1: 14, that there are aneles sent from God to protect those who will come to believe in him before they die. Nowhere, can I find any scriptural references telling us if they stay or go after we have been "saved". The Bible repeatedly informs us that when/if we come to the point in our personal life, that we accept God's provision for attaining a heavenly eternity, that we receive God's own Holy Spirit (Ephesians 1: 16 and many more verses) to guarantee our abode with God when we pass. He does that, in referencing our "new found" condition, as being like a child, who despite all else can never change our birth heritage. Change you name, or where you live, or anything else; your parents are STILL *Your* parents.

That all being said; I have one more-(ya) one more (at least) "guardian angel type story." Hey what do I call it otherwise? So it's another beautiful summer weekday in Southeast Wisconsin, and I am heading back home to the suburb of Milwaukee where I lived, called Greenfield. Of course it is on the "other side" of downtown, so yes each morning and each afternoon I get to go through our congested traffic conditions. Now, that very large and wide six cylinder touring bike, (Kawasaki Voyager 1300), was so smooth and comfortable to go that long distance twice a day, but in the heavy traffic, nothing is fun to ride. That bike wasn't much smaller than say maybe half of an automobile in a lane space just shorter. Let's simply say "it is bigger than a "smart car," and probably as heavy, So it commanded a lot of area on the road; for being a large mostly black motorcycle, and of course lovely to look at too; especially if you're stuck in a car.

Please remember, I am somebody who has lived and died on my Kawasaki; so cut me some slack, will ya? Thanks.

OK!

Therefore, I am now driving home from Sheboygan, and almost get to the heaviest congested part of the freeway, going in the middle of the three lanes about forty miles an hour (along with all the traffic) and as you approach downtown Milwaukee, there is an "S" curve that curves its way along to the middle of town.

Sweeping to the right to continue going south and now a little to the west, everything was going along quite smoothly, even with all of the cars, almost bumper to bumper. Then as all of the traffic made the rolling left curve to continue south, I suddenly look out the corner of my eye inside my full face helmet, and saw a full size car choosing to obliterate my presence in that center lane, as it veered quickly to the left, right towards my right shoulder.

Close to a "panic" reaction move, I cut (to the left) into the lane that had a large utility truck and car immediately in front and next to me. Sincerely leaving me No Where to Go! I somehow slipped between the car and truck directly in front of me and to my left.

It could only have been a "miraculous" move by say, my guardian angel that squeezed that fiberglass surrounded touring bike mere inches from both cars now parallel with me for about five or six more car lengths. The look on those two drivers may have even caused them to believe in some form of heavenly power.

Chapter Seven

You *will* Really Get A "Charge" out of This!

{B+} Not a Bad Grade

One afternoon, while I was still up in Sheboygan, one of my "loyal" Friday night *Young Adult Bible Studies attendee's (The one* that has now been going on for twelve years;) called me and asked me if I would be interested in a Job, down closer to my house in the Milwaukee area? "Sure..." I quickly replied. The two hour's *plus* just driving to Sheboygan and back is getting real hard to tolerate sometimes. But wait, {what kind of Job Is It?}" I besought him.

"Dave, he proceeded, you know that I have worked here at *Batteries Plus* for close to a year now and they are really expanding, and looking for store managers with retail experience." "Ok-go on." Well they are opening a new store up in West Allis in a couple of months. (It's a close Suburb of Milwaukee).

He went on "You'd be the perfect guy for that job and place." "Thanks Tom. I guess I could check it out." So he gave me the phone number, and I called." This Tom was also the fella who

got to my Emergency room visit before anyone else, too. He is a
Great Friend.

They hired me right after the president of the company interviewed me. He just couldn't understand why I would want a job
like that, with all my religious training and degrees. They wanted
me to open a brand new location for them in a busy suburb just
west of Milwaukee.

I could write a whole book just on the adventure that took
place for those nine years that I was corporate store manager, there.

I was pretty much left in total control of inventory and
employees, and that alone was a full time job, but it was perpet-
ually interesting, to say the least. By the way; where did All of the
Differences come from in all livings. Plant, animal, cold blooded
warm blooded? The "Big Bang" brought us all of that too? hmm

I was just coming around the corner from outside on the
parking lot at the Batteries plus store in West Allis, on one afternoon day, when I approached the open trunk-lid of an employee
who had been working there for about six months. He was the
third person in all of those years that "corporate" made me hire
him, which I wasn't in preference of.

He happened to be putting a case of four hundred AA batteries in his car to take home with him, when his shift was over,
in about ten minutes. To say the least he was extremely startled
to see me standing there watching him. He stuttered to try to say
that he was delivering them to a customer. When I asked him
to then show me the invoice, he reached back in to the trunk;
handed me the batteries, got in his car and was never seen again
by anybody from Batteries Plus.

We also had the opportunity to almost make our store to be the first with a "drive through." A very old woman was pulling up to the front of the store, which had a raised sidewalk going directly across the front of the building. There was a cart with big meters and hand tools for exchanging car batteries. Suddenly the whole left front of the glass and brick building were scattered all around the complete inside of the building when she accidently hit the gas pedal instead of the brake. Her car finally stopped about three feet inside the building, hitting a pegboard wall of camcorder batteries. Whey! That got our attention alright.

Thankfully; nobody got hurt or injured, especially the older woman driver or customers. Then, trying to explain all that to corporate headquarters and that we had a car literally *in* our store, which needed some serious building repair, and definitely before we closed that night.

The most interesting story that took place in "my-the" store, happened to be when a mid-thirties something black fella started working for me. I interviewed him and recommended him to corporate who vetted him, as a qualified person. He was doing really well for about four or five months, and telling me how he would really like to be a store manager someday. He was a good hard worker and tall, so he could reach anything we needed.

As I told him, his potential, in customer service, tech training, and his promptness and attendance at work was showing great signs of his being able to someday become a manager of a corporate store, as they kept expanding all over the country at a healthy pace.

He usually worked from noon to closing at eight pm. The two cash drawers were always balanced well. Strangely, one day things were going a little slower and none of us paid much attention to the clock. Two men in suit and ties (just like men in black) entered the store. It really made us question their stiff and tense behavior. Because really, few people come into our Battery store, all dressed up, but hey that was how they were. (again- to each their own?)

One of the fellas briskly, came up to the service counter and asked to speak to the owner or manager. I responded that, it was me. Urgently he asked if {we'll call my employee John Brown} was worked here. I instantly snapped back with a "yes he does; why?" The quick reply wasn't an answer, but rather "is he here now?" I promptly came back with, "NO- he's not in yet, why, what do you need him for?"

Reaching into their suit coat pockets, they each pulled out a small billfold, and opening them simultaneously to reveal FBI agent badges.

"Your, Mr. John Brown, robbed a local credit union branch a couple of hours ago, and we have his picture on our cameras, and he was wearing a green Batteries Plus work polo shirt. Which made his identification very quick and easy to find."

"He WHATTT?" We all cried out together. They came back with "As soon as they opened, he walked in with a paper bag in his hand, and threatened the teller to give him all the money in her drawer."

Each one placing a business card on the front counter; They then each turned and were rapidly headed back to the front door, when one turned and sternly barked "If he comes in or you see him anywhere, you better call us right away." "Got that?"

We three nodded in rather frightened agreement, and I headed for the telephone to call corporate, yet again. See, Batteries Plus corporate headquarters were about twenty miles west of our store, and many of the employees and or their family and friends, would come in to our store, often, either to shop or just keep an eye on us, for corporate.

With no real right to brag, I do want to tell you this, that after just five and a half years, the Batteries Plus-West Allis, WI. Became the nation's largest corp. store. As the back cover shows; It obviously wasn't accomplished on my good looks, but rather customers that I had from the *Oak Creek MotorSports* days, and all of the new *Batteries Plus* customers that spread the word, that we WILL take care of our customers. The word spread that I was running that store, and they came to me to get the most honest batteries (be it for heavy equipment or apartment complexes, or just a watch battery, etc.)

I was raised with the adage;" Lie to me once and ask yourself when is the next time that I should believe you?" YES! Honesty really does pay. Every year that I worked for Batteries Plus they had to change their manager bonus program, because I quite often overdid their parameters. But they didn't just give me "nice" large bonuses but rather at least annually or sometimes bi-annually when we did inventory of the "gazillion" batteries that we had in stock. There was one sometimes two corp. exec-utives who "helped" with our inventory, usually till the "wee" hours of the morning. They simply couldn't believe our numbers. But YES they were accurate ad real. In my mind/heart, GOD gets the glory for that.

One interesting business condition that I used, was to teach my employees in the store just how to sell something to the customer; not to make the sale, but how to show the customer the value in what you are trying to convince them to purchase.

For example; <u>Batteries Plus</u> offered a "W.F.W"., which stood for "Worry Free Warranty". When a customer purchased the highest grade auto battery for their vehicle they became qualified to purchase a warranty that would persist for at least ten years. Now that is way longer than almost any street-use batteries will last.

After incentivizing my employees with things like Dairy Queen Blizzard and special parties for the store's outstanding performance, they started informing the customers to such a level that when I tell you this, you won't believe it either.

Prior to my arrival, the average <u>Batteries Plus</u> store sold 3 ½ W.F.W. in a year. Bringing in about $35.00 additional. After the second year the Batteries Plus- West Allis, had sold 10,000.00 W.F.W.s, YES! really. In just one year. It was nothing other than a big PLUS for all involved. Customer re-assurance, the stores bottom line, and Corporates value. Take note that there were no "inventory costs there either."

A great story of incentivizing employees, was when I first started to manage the Batteries Plus West Allis store. I found out about a "type of "batteries for cars truck motorcycles etc. that was called "Odyssey." It is So powerful because of its design and size and most of all hat even though it goes into all of these different vehicle, I is "dry" so It can't spill or leak damaging the unit. The only little "quirk" (is that even a word?). The battery cost almost two times the price of a typical battery it would replace. It did howere, last much much longer and have more power and not harm equipment.

I learned a lot about them and even tried one in one of my own motorcycles. WOW Is that an awesome battery. So I started offering my employees some incentives to sell them; which of course they all thought that I was a little "nut," thinking that people would spend that much for a battery.

But after showing them some videos, and training them on how to sell those batteries, one would go out here and there. As time went on, my counter working employees got more comfortable presenting them to customers because of their exceptionally long warranties. More and more of them were getting sold each month. So I increase the incentive from a blizzard to some really cool items, like leather jackets, multi-tooled knife kits, different computer accessories, and the like.]

Here is where it gets interesting too. The average Batteries Plus store across the country; at the time sold maybe one or two a year. After the first full year, we had already sold sixty of them. That got corporates attention, for sure. The second and third year, we were in the low to mid one hundreds.

Then one spring, when Hardley was having their "100 Year birthday party, up here in Milwaukee, Wis. I ordered over 100 at one time almost exclusively for motorcycles. They all came in and we were selling the heck out of them when a B+ corporate "big shot" came in to the store in a real "dither." His words to me went like this: "Did you order almost $10,000. Odyssey's last month? I smiled and said "Yup sure did" "WWhhaaTT?" was his screeching response, which also included "are You Crazy?" All I could say was NOPE" How are you ever going to sell all of those?" Came right back. I just looked and said that almost a third of them are gone already." "That's good, but that's only a third." Calmly I said. "Yes, and wait and see when their all gone." "You "damn-well" better hope so snapped back at me.

By the end of summer we were almost all out of them. And my employees all got some really nice rewards. We even did something very unique for a *Batteries Plus* store. We had a nice big fun exclusive dinner. The key, I believe, was that I showed real appreciation to my employee's for their exceptional performance. I guess that is what led so many other store employees, want to work at our store.

On Christmas, I gave a relatively new employee, (who we had learned, didn't have much of any kind of family life.) a real special gift. Because he was trying so hard at work and doing such a fine job, and kept the inventory and money in good standing during his hours. I handed him a brand new Odyssey insulated leather jacket. After his surprise, we couldn't find him anywhere. Then I opened one back door, and there he was sitting on the ground weeping.

I asked, "What's wrong?" don't you like It?" "NO NO ! I love it. But Nobody has ever given me a gift anything like this before. This is the greatest gift I ever got from somebody." Then I got squeezed in such a hard bear hug, you just couldn't imagine. Things like that, sure make life feel good.

Going *INTERSTATE* while at home

Funny how things go, but when you do "good", at one place {good} seems to follow you. Here's an example of what I mean by that. Suddenly out of nowhere one day my telephone at home rang; I answered it and found that the call was from one of the

Vice Presidents from *Interstate Battery Corp.* out of Dallas Texas. They were impressed with their competition (*Batteries Plus*) corporate store performance in the West Allis, Wisconsin location. Someone had given them my card and they knew that I was in charge of that location.

My battery knowledge and success in sales, and experience in management, somehow got me connected with another battery company; some of you readers may have heard of. It is known as *Interstate Battery Corporation.* Yup; the big car battery company. Whose lime green (obvious Kawasaki colors) *NASCAR* race car, is seen all over the country and on video. Well, actually they were already in the "retail battery business." They had purchased another version of *Batteries Plus* that had started in Des Moines Iowa, about ten years earlier. Interstate was now ready to "take off."

I had talked with one of the Vise Presidents for almost two hours, in the space of a week.

He then invited me down to the Corporate headquarter in Dallas, Texas. A few weeks later, I took a flight down and spent the day meeting all of the execs. The next day I flew home, and in two days, was sent a very nice job offer. For the next six years I managed the upper-Midwest stores scattered around Michigan and Illinois. After they had sold those locations to franchisee's, I stayed in the Milwaukee are, handling all of Southeast Wisconsin, dealer accounts.

After about five years, I was told that our huge regional territory had the most "retail battery sales in the company's corporate stores, nation-wide.

<u>Triumphant!</u>

The "Great Recession" hit in 2008 and all companies "pulled in their horns," likewise with *Interstate Batteries*. So there was no position for working for them at that juncture. I felt close to retiring anyhow, until I called a telephone number for someone looking for old & classic motorcycles. After a few descriptive answers to the questions of what I had, they made an appointment to come to my house and see what I all had for sale.

Upon his arrival a few days later, I immediately recognized the gentleman, who was one of the two brothers who owned the car dealerships that I spoke of earlier. He looked at what I had, then told me of their plans to open up a <u>Triumph</u> motorcycle dealership, and it was only a few blocks from my residence.

So there I am again, managing a motorcycle dealership on 27th St. once more. Strangest thing was, we were stuck in an "out lot" building right in the middle of the auto lot. Not to obvious or noticeable. The fascinating information that I had received a little over the first year, was that the one girl that I had helping me sell; whose name was Aricka had done close to the impossible. We sold those new Triumph's and used cycles and ATV's. We were told that we had sold close to <u>double</u> the amount of new Triumph's that we were expected to. All of the demographic information that they had about us was wrong. And it was in our opening year, that's what *Triumph Motors* told the new dealership. (My "good looks"? probably Arica's.)

I now ask you to please DO Not, think that all of these First's, Number One's, and Nation's largest achievements were attained to, just by me skills or savvy salesmanship, or "cheapest price.

Rather, as I know and hope you will come to accept, is that it was done by God's grace and mercy, and the training that HE saw that I needed. The real point behind both this and the first book, is not to garner adulation or praise, but to give it to my Savior and God.

MILES from Home

Life, for the Dave Miles' family was going along pretty steady for the rest of the nineties. Both of our boys were enrolled in a private "Christian based" grade/high school called *Heritage Christian,* and they got a fantastic education, and were able to be involved in a lot of different sports, as well.

My oldest son Eric, graduated from Heritage High School, then enrolled into the University of Wisconsin Parkside- campus. He spent two years there, while living with us at home. The school was about twenty miles from our house, so he could keep his expenses down.

Eric, who is just "one a great guy" and a wonderful son, had several outside jobs, for school, books, gas money and for his personal activities, (Usually friends and movies.) After the first two years he decided to attend The University of Wisconsin-Milwaukee. It was a lot closer and he could still live in the base-ment {cost free}. What makes me so proud, is that he got all of his education paid for real quick. So for the rest of his life he is not burdened by that awful student loan debt that so unfortunately "haunts" so many college students. Remember; I'm a (volunteer) financial counselor. Maybe some of it rubbed off.

What really made me and his mother ecstatic, was his decision to go on a six week, shall we say "sabbatical"? But the reason is so awesome. He went on a mission trip to the Philippine's to spend time with a family stationed there and take in the country. He also got to go to Manila, to meet some rather "well off" folks that my parents knew.

When he came home, he was loaded with a huge array of interesting stories. Like when he kept asking if we would enjoy "chicken Adidas?" Chicken...what? We asked. Chicken "adidas." He replied. "What the heck is that?" His brother, mother and I questioned. "Chicken feet...!" of course like the shoes Adidas." "Riighhtt! Three little bitty claws; for food?" The people over in the Philippine's love them and enjoy how they taste. All I could say after that was, "Sure saves on toothpicks... I guess"

Our youngest son Timothy also graduated from *Heritage Christian High,* several years later. He is simply "So-smart" especially in math. His mother and her sister {ya Tim's aunt} are all really good in all of "those" math courses. It sure didn't come from my side, even though my mom is so financially astute.

Tim is so smart and, that in high school, that he took all the {A.P.} courses that he could. So when he chose to attend Carthage College, down in Kenosha, Wisconsin, He was able to acquire numerous Grants and he even tested out of a whole semester of classes; Which enabled him to finish college with his B.A. and be ready for job offers way before his other class-mates.

"Merry Ole' England"

I was also privileged to go to England with my son, Tim, who was still finishing high school at *Heritage Christian* School; when he was about 16 or so. We encountered all kinds of adventures from of our visit. Our first ride on the "Tube" was a real frightening experience {for me, that is}.

We were going down the several groups of stairs after we had decided to head downtown. London is a very big old city. We were staying in an old multi storied hotel. It was about six to eight miles west of the old original city. Our agreement was to get off, as close to Parliament, as we could get. Then as we are approaching the bottom set of stairs, Tim saw and called to me that, the cars with the right number was about to leave.

He hurried down those stairs real adolescent quickly, and got in between the doors just as I was approaching the door way. The only thing was, I wasn't as quick as he was, and I was unable to make it before the doors slammed shut, and that subway train started to take off down the tracks, very quickly leaving me stranded on the platform.

The only problem was, I had no idea, how far he was going to go before getting off, so we could meet back up. Being so unfamiliar with all of this, and not having pre-arranged any contingency for where we would meet if we got separated, but there was a huge lump growing in my stomach. While waiting for the next train with the correct numbers, I mulled to myself. Does he even know the way back to the hotel that we were staying at? Does he have any money (pounds) to get back to this station? How will I ever find him again?

Now, he is really smart, and the worst part is that he is a lot smarter than his father (Ya me). How will he think this through? Do I get off at the first stop, or go all the way downtown, and try to find him there? I wasn't panicked, but close to it. So I decided to get on the next one and get off at the very next station and see if he did, also.

But what if he gets off and comes back and I'm not here? I could just imagine going right past him in the wrong direction. I hope that this next comment won't surprise you, but I did urgently start to pray. It felt like another eon of time passing, but I waited out at our original point of departure, till another tram came with the right number and see if he just came back. When the train stopped to let people off and on, a lot of folks exited the car, but... Wait! It's him there he is! "Praise the LORD!" Was all that I could say, for that one.

Around the <u>GLOBE</u>... in an Hour

Good thing I wasn't any older, 'cause he may have come back and seen this "old guy" laying on the deck from a heart attack. But when the next train came with the number we needed, we boarded together, and went all of the way to the river Thames, and then we toured the whole part of the old city that was so interesting to both of us. He was so long legged and well built, he could out-do me at almost everything. Hey but that's what I was proud of.

We visited the Tower of London Bridge, with the famous "Beefeaters", and to the perfect {almost round} replica of the

Shakespearian play-house, named the "GLOBE." See we did get around the "Globe" in about an hour (ha-ha).

On another adventure a few days later, we took a passenger train ride up into the countryside of England. We got off and flagged a taxi that would take us to a place called "Bourdon on the Waters." Some locals that lived down in London suggested it to us, about how beautiful it was and still rather "quaint."

The other very interesting thing that we learned, was while we waited for about forty-five minutes in a little five or six building town, where the train dropped us off. We thought we would get some lunch. Finding a sign hanging out in front of one of the building on the end of town, looking like it was a type of let's say "eatery;" I opened the door and was welcomed in while noticing just a couple of tables, in the whole little room.

While sitting at our table the older gentleman asked what we would like. He insinuated that he knew we were going to order a couple of "pints." After asking for a menu, and gazing at the very very limited offering, we decided to be adventurous some more and order, what many people in England (so we're told) just love to east; which was a no-mayonnaise covered cucumber sandwich. It was something that wouldn't be put on our table at home, but I raised both boys, that if or when they travel, they should at least "give the local cuisine and some customs a try."

All in all, it was a great trip, and we both had a lot of fun. Even when we visited Harrods's department store, and got to see the memorial for Princess Diana. That the owner of Harrods's erected in the store for his "daughter-in-law" the princess.

"Bushmills" or bust!

A couple of years after our younger son, Tim & I, took our English excursion, I got the opportunity, once again, to go to Ireland with my oldest son, Eric. It was another "trip of a lifetime for two fellas, {father and son) who wanted to be somewhat "adventurous".

We landed in Shannon, and rented a car to take us through-out the whole country. Out of the airport we headed straight for the Cliffs of Moher, and Eric, who is an avid photographer, couldn't wait to get there. But first we had to load our luggage and things into the rental car, which was rather small, due to the roads in Ireland being very narrow, sometimes almost "channel-like", with no room for even a ditch.

I will say this though, that between our two bodies and our gear, we and the cargo baaareely fit. We did finally get ourselves and everything in, and then contend with the steering wheel on the "wrong-side" aaacch! Once "all in" we headed (nowhere near straight) to the cliffs.

Wow, the country roads down in the southwest part of Ireland bend and roll with the terrain, but not a problem, until another car or "heaven for bid" one of their big utility trucks, would be coming right for us. Yikes! It was really a tight squeeze, to say the least. See, that for hundreds and hundreds of years, farmers in those country plots of land, used all of the rocks and stone that came up year after year on the farm fields, as fences; literally "right next to the road." They seemed to all be about three feet or so high, and maybe a couple of feet wide, not allowing any traffic to have some mercy when on-coming vehicles weres part of the equation.

We would almost come to a complete stop, and nudge our little car as close to the rocks as we dare. Thankfully no collisions, but I was sure glad that I had bought the extra insurance. Whew!

The Cliffs were fabulous, but we had a lot more of Ireland to see. We went to Kilkenny, and to the neatest little park, named "Powers Court" with its own waterfall. It was sort of hidden in a nice woods, and a lot of the locals didn't even know about it.

Waterford is an awesome city where all of that gorgeous crystal is made and cut so intricately beautiful. And when we arrived at Dublin; surprise! My son loves different beers, and of course if you like beer you WILL Love Guinness, dark stout. Just think, that brewery is older than the United States is a nation. NO, not the beer we drank.

After a couple of days in town, we ventured out to the north and west. We worked our way towards the city of Galway, and then over to the part known as Northern Ireland.

It is hard to imagine the same island, the same countryside, but when you entered Northern Ireland by car, you could have sworn that you just drove right into England proper itself. It was so lovely up there, and later that afternoon we arrived up at the very top of the country, where there is a section protruding into the Atlantic Ocean known as the "Giants Causeway." It is so amazing all of the large and totally flat stones protruding just above the water line, like a sidewalk, heading towards Scotland.

Enough of that already, my son wanted to get to Bushmill's distillery. Not knowing the hour of tours or any of their scheduling, we found that the next tour would be in an hour or so. We casually walked around the beautiful grounds, and then sat at a little gazebo where we waited.

Sometimes, despite my big mouth, we can get good information. A gardener fella was walking by and I asked him just where we should go to get to the start of the tour of the distillery.

Probably for the sake of somebody to talk to, he proceeded to inform us of where and when to be for the beginning of the next tour. Then as a total surprise to the two of us, he asked "Do you want the best part of the tour?" "Sure," We responded. "Well then," in his distinct Irish brogue, he started to hunch over the little bench we were sitting on, like this would be the biggest secret of the century. "Stay close behind the tour guide, and when they take you into the "tasting room," be as close as possible and as soon as he starts to talk, {Raise Your Hand}." "OK" we replied.

"You see, he is going to pick the first five people who raise their hands, to be the "taste-testers" for that particular tour group. They will each get 5 different whiskeys to test, to see which one is the best, of course we all hope that they will choose Bushmills, as their favorite." That was a secret that my son truly wanted to know.

The time came for our tour to gather and follow the guide. It was a fascinating tour of how they distill Bushmills whiskey, and as we were close to finish the tour, we came into a type of "Pub" atmosphere room. The tour guide thanked us all for coming and hoped that we enjoyed the tour. As he took another breath, to begin his final statement, my son rapidly put his arm up, and as the guide was sweeping his view around himself finishing an invitation, he was made clearly aware that this young man was volunteering.

To say the least, he was one of the five picked for the final "taste test." He sure did enjoy the tour of Bushmills distillery, and for some strange reason, we then felt little remorse in purchasing one of their one hundred year old bottles that they made available for us to purchase.

Go *East* Young Man- Go *East*!

In 1998 my mom found a super deal for traveling to Thailand. After the very severe collapse of the Asian economy in 1997 everything was pretty "cheap." So my dad and I went off to Bangkok, Thailand for a ten day vacation.

After an excruciating eighteen hour flight, landing in Hawaii, then Hong Kong, finally we got to the Suvarnabhumi Airport. The shuttle bus ride to the hotel seemed almost as long as the flight. The city with its buildings and population felt like it was almost endless. I have been in many different cities around the world, but this metropolis puts all others to shame as far as square miles covered.

We finally arrived downtown at a huge skyscraper Hilton hotel. Once we checked in and went to the room and received our luggage; because it was early enough in the day and we had been doing nothing but sitting for almost a full day; we decided to go for a short walk.

Maybe, a few blocks from the hotel, there was a long high bridge straddling a very large river, and it was busy with all sorts of marine traffic. The name of this busy-wide- fast moving river is Chao Phraya. (Ya, I can't properly pronounce it either).

As we approached the foot of the bridge, we noticed numerous amounts of people with cane-poles, fishing over the side (good thing they were fishing over the side-no?). Surmising that it might be a sign of a good day's catch, we proceeded to walk up the sidewalk portion by the railing. That is where we looked into the (whattt??-river)! All that could be seen was solid deep dark brown, as if it were pure mud. Turning to my father, I queried "How could a fish even see a hook or any bait?" His horizontal head shake back and forth clued me to his response. After seeing that, we both agreed that we weren't probably going to order any seafood, while in Thailand.

The really cool thing that we did avidly watch, was the long "river boats." They were motoring up and down the river, and parking all over on each bank. But what was so fascinating to us was the twenty foot long propeller shaft, with a blade protruding at the end, but the real interesting part was how they moved down the river. The outboard motor was a small cylinder car engine that had a steering bar/handle like a typical fishing motor. The driver would hold on like it was a 9.9 hp. outboard, just the difference was this was a real fast and "ultra" loud auto engine. Those things were really cool.

The boats themselves were rather long and narrow, as well as having a real shallow draft. We were informed that they are called "LONG TAIL" boats. Just make sure you stay away from the end of that tail

The next morning we got on a tourist bus and were given a great view of the city itself. As the morning went on we arrived by the big 'brown" river and were escorted onto a rather large river boat. We then proceeded up the river and out of the city general itself.

Having been around boats and motorboats especially, I must confess that this was one really weird ride that we took, for about twenty minutes or so, until we came to a brightly decorated gorgeously styled oriental building with a boarding dock. We all jettisoned the long tail boat, and went in to the very "open air" banquet hall. There we were served a fabulous dinner, of which I couldn't tell you what almost any of it was. But boy was it tasty.

"I'M Gonna Die…!

The following day, we got "courageous" and decided to take a little tour of our own. We went down to the lobby and stepped out the front, and saw numerous little three wheel mini-bikes with a little canopy top, and a two person back seat. Realizing that those were the primary taxis, we stepped further towards the road.

My father stepped in and sat down, as I put my right leg into the unit, the driver hit the gas and proceeded to take off. One big problem there, I was really still standing on the sidewalk, when he dashed into traffic. I was fortunate enough to have my right hand gripping onto the vertical canopy support, but the bulk of my body and weight were still back on the pavement. Had I let go right then, I would have fallen forward and been run over the next "tuk-tuk" waiting for a fare.

My dad heard my yelp, and leaned over to grab my elbow, while I was proclaiming "I'm gonna Die." That eruption did little to slow the "tuk-tuk" driver down.

To this day I really have NO Idea, how I was able to get myself in, but when I sat down I held on tight. Are you starting see why I am a firm believer in providential care? So far, it has worked really well.

Made In.. (to) China

In the early part of the new Twenty-First century my mom found once again a great deal on a trip to China. My father was always fascinated with the "Great Wall" and in his late seventies, he almost thought that was something that he would never get to experience. But I was able to make my schedule work so my dad and I got on a plane and took off for the Asian continent, once again.

We landed in Shanghai, and toured the large city, then we got to fly out across the country to *Xi`an*, where the *"Terra Cotta"* warriors were discovered. Just a short history blurb. In 1972 when Hank and I got to go to Japan, Taiwan, then Hong Kong, we saw a lot of the Eastern Hemisphere. Back then we toured the various islands that comprise Hong Kong, we came to some cliffs on the mainland and huge fences going across the terrain. The guide pointed and told us that, what we were looking at, was the nation of Communist China, and if we were to go up and over that fence we would be immediately shot. Now less than thirty years later, we are flying all over that country; somewhat open and free. But not totally. Lots of police and military guards all around.

Those Terra Cotta warriors and their chariots were so impressively interesting and almost unbelievable, that they had only been discovered some nine years earlier. It was just so astronomical in quantity and individuality, you could hardly believe that they were thousands of years old.

Going to the "Great Wall' and seeing the size, length and scope was truly awe inspiring, as well. China is a very unique country, culture, and atmosphere. The amount of traffic in Beijing, it makes L.A. look like a farm community of drivers.

We also spent several days touring Beijing. It sure is an interestingly large and very busy city. They were getting ready for the winter OLYMPICS, that were going to happen in a year.

Then it became another very long flight home, but we spent a lot of it reminiscing all of our sights, sounds, and flavors. We were even taught that over 98 % of all "Chinese restaurants" in America, come from the province of China, called Canton. The tour guide told us that their food flavoring was so much more delectable, and that they tend to have much more flavorful food that we Westerners really enjoy in their various cuisines.

Is Don really that <u>ODE</u>?

Having talked about my dad a lot in these later chapters; I felt that it was important for you readers, to get to know him a little better.

Born in Burlington Wisconsin, and later as a boy, his parents and siblings moved to the near west side of Milwaukee. At age sixteen, he got himself into the Army-Air Force, which was still a rather new branch of the military.

After boot camp, he along with thousands of others were shipped off to war. His ship and duty were headed to Europe. Two days out of dock in France, the war came to an official end.

Not that all of the snipers and some avid German soldiers, had all accepted that fact. He worked for a colonel, who started arranging, all of the 'logistical' challenges of closing down the war. The colonel and my dad built a friendship which then back in "the states" developed into the and our family going around America to visit each other.

Here is a poem/Ode that I wrote for him when he and another friend Don Clark, were invited by a volunteer organization, which actually began in a suburb of Milwaukee, called Port Washington. They were amongst hundreds of WWII soldiers that got to take a special "Honor Flight" to Washington D.C. to finally get to see the war memorial for the "Greatest Generation."

We took them down to the Milwaukee Airport, early in the morning, then when the plane was full, it took off to D.C. and they were bused to the big new war memorial, and were served lunch and even got to go to the "Tomb of the Unknown Soldier."

143

When they were brought back later in that late afternoon, they were met by all of the family and friends as they walked, or many wheeled, up the concourse. We jumped and hollered and waved flags, and gave them all a welcome that they had never imagined.

I don't think that there was a dry eye in the building. A few weeks earlier, the families were all contacted to bring some form of honoring memorabilia for the soldiers that they were taking home.

That is why I wrote this ODE to my father. Which Is true to my heart. My son & daughter in law, along with my mom and wife all joyfully greeted him and we tried to find a little quieter area off to the side.

I pulled out a little scroll, and read the Ode to my dad. It appeared to move him emotionally, which (by the way) I had never seen in my entire life, before.

His Irish heritage must have given it to him, because for as long as I can remember he has written poems and proclamations for other people's special occasions, like weddings, and birthdays.

Here is my heart opening up to my Father.

Ode to Donald Miles

Faithful to the LORD...Faithful to Your land (USA)
Faithful to Your wife & son...
And Faithful to all most everyone.

Deserving of all the honor & Respect, We can give...
With your loyalty to all: We can safely live

Responsible... You Are!
And needed time, you'll spend
No Greater a servant...no Greater a Friend.

To help out another, plus...thru to the end
No firmer Foundation...the Miles name, can send

A legacy, O'Fine... To the highest degree
Only shame & disgust will be certain, to flee

The Miles name be Proud & Stalwart can stand
That all who Know it...Can take rest, in that hand

A future home...& One, that's well... Here
Will be complete... With just a book & a beer.

What makes me so sad, to say, is... Why do we *WAIT* to praise, honor, and respect individuals, in our lives, until after they have passed? Why don't we give them the personal accolades, and honor while they are still with us?

The picture below is, my father when he had just joined the U.S. Army/Air Force. It is pretty obvious why my mom married him. He was quite the "looker," huh? Which makes me wonder If I wasn't maybe really adopted, or switched in the nursery.

I was born in Milwaukee, Wisconsin,

1. I don't like beer

2. I don't care for the Brewers

3. I have little interest in the Green Bay Packers

4. And it should be quite apparent, that I have no love for a motorcycle who claims to be made in the U.S.A.

But this man in the picture taught me well. When he said, "David… Remember this {To each their own} and don't forget it. Share what you believe to be right or the best, but let everyone make up their own mind. Got that?" My simple reply was "Yup."

Life Goes ON?

As we all know; life after "9-11" changed all of us in the United States. For the next few years, none of us knew what was next, or what to expect that life was to be like in the future. My years at Batteries Plus had granted me some vacation time that I had never know before. As I shared in the first book, way back in 1966 when "we" at Oak Creek MotorSports began selling snowmobiles and motorcycles, we began selling a type of camping trailer known as a "Pop-Up". That's what the company way up in northern Wisconsin was doing before we took on their snowmobiles.

With our proximity to Milwaukee, and all of busy Southeastern Wisconsin, they urged us to take on their campers as well. So Hank did, and now were in the RV business too.

About two years after we were married, (Elsbeth and I that is) the two of us bought one of the campers. We didn't get a lot of time to use it, but it was "Kinda" fun, and we made the most of it. The only thing that was a huge void in my life of camping was; "here we are up in the beautiful north woods and enjoying God's ambience of nature," but what can we do besides go hiking, or maybe off shore fishing? Here is where I must make a big confession: I can only sing "KUMBYA" so many times at the campfire. "Sorry Lord."

It was almost like new, and in perfect shape, so I sold the camper, a couple of years later. I thought that probably ended our camping chapter of life. Was I wrong! No, we didn't start a new phase with "He holds the Whole World in His Hands" either. I had been saying repeatedly "why don't they make a way, so a person could take a cycle or ATV" One day while I was at Batteries Plus, a large and long diesel pick-up truck pulled into our large easy access corner parking lot. It was pulling a long and high camping trailer. The customer need two new batteries that fit into a little outer compartment. They had to be the "deep cycle" type for the camper's lights.

I sold him the two specific batteries and because we offered "free installation, with purchase," I carried them out and waited for him to show me where they went. As I was mounting and wiring them the customer and I started talking about the camper (the one that is now taking up most of our customer parking area.

He told me that it is called a "toy hauler." "A what?" I queried. The back of the camper is like a garage, that you can put things like motorcycles or ATV's in. WOW! Now that sounded interesting. So after the batteries were all mounted and wired; he took me on a little tour. "Now this is Awesome" I sort of blurted out. This is how camping should be. He then gave me my parking lot back and we waved good-bye to one another. And I am now "stoked."

After finding an almost new dually-diesel pickup truck Elsbeth and I started shopping all over the upper-Midwest looking at numerous camping stores for a nice maybe used "toy-hauler." Finally after shopping for almost a year, we found one that seemed just right for us. And it would let us take along our family and have a great time in up north Wisconsin camping and ATVing.

If you have never driven a semi-truck and trailer, you will be able to empathize with me, when I tell you of my "great apprehension, leaving the camping store dealership. How far to go out into the road before turning so you don't put the trailer in the ditch or on the curb, and then to try that trick when turning to the right, where you really can't see what's going on. Let me tell you, now, over 10 years later and thousands of miles pulling our much bigger and longer toy hauler, which we purchased a few years later; only because it had a much longer and bigger "garage allowing us to take two more ATV's with us. I have learned how it tows so nice and easy and backs in to the camp site very well, but did it ever take the practice. (Oh) and in my case a lot of prayer, as well.

Hurray! After all of those years, telling customers how much fun, that they could have on their Kawasaki's, my wife and I, along with some of our family finally got our chance at enjoying the outdoors as well

"Champagne or Beer... Sir?"

My point behind telling you all of this, has been to reinforce my comments about how short life might be, and try to make the most of it while you can. But also, as I share to all of the people who come to me for free financial counsel (because I volunteer for the *Crown Financial Ministries* organization) each of us *Must* be diligent and disciplined enough to budget our incomes to our "out-go." My maternal grandpa, sat me down one day, when I was probably about twelve or thirteen, and said, "David, remember one thing. You can't keep drinking champagne on a beer budget. Just remember that" "Yes grandpa" I replied. It got the message across, to me. Just look at all of that sage advice; that I had received.

Chapter Eight

"The Past IS — *Present!*...again"

Here now, just inches away, from impingement, with an "aged' deeply wrinkled almost "scar-ish" face, pocked by horror and extreme fear; this very very old woman's expression of panic, exuding from her frozen glare looked shuttering enough with those eyes to even scare me by that alone. We were now so close to each other's face that I could see all of this, in her driver's windows; which I was about to instantly intrude. And this, all in the reflection of my helmet's face shield. I could clearly see just now, that I had a similar look of horror and fright simultaneously on my own petrified stare. The motorcycle's headlight now like a beacon glaring against the door and window glass, stared right into her driver's door side and window. I surely knew once more, that this was really "gonna" hurt. Then came the inevitable crash! "NO...!" I silently screamed, to myself. And at that instant I slammed right into her driver's door, with the entire force of the front of my motorcycle. Meanwhile I found myself staring at that huge "door mounted" chrome mirror that looked like IT was coming right at my throat. Past the front fender, the front wheel, the "wrap around" fairing, with windshield and signal lights all previously in place. Next was my bike's set of gauges that were in place on light rubber mounts. The pod of meters, instantly snapped off and slip down the gas tank (front to back) and shortly rested right in my lap.

Decoratively robotic enough, I started my contorted acrobatic flailing "routine,"once again, which sent me all over that big intersection again. ONLY, this time I didn't go unconscious or die like my first aileron gyrations.

With nothing but an almost pitch-black starlight night sky, and some headlights, horizontally trying to pierce the dark; I felt myself lofting through the air. Believe it or not time felt like it stood still." I could see myself 'swirling around and noticed the business lights coming and going; even the street lights and the red and green traffic flashes. It was just like being on a Ferris wheel. While accelerating upward, {I sensed} I was able to start a conversation with GOD! My quote "Ya" better get ready, 'cause here I come!"

WHAM! I severely collided with something? I felt the "hit," but not the hurt? Hood? Roof? Trunk? Asphalt? All that I knew upon impact was that I hit something real hard. And then I bounced (really I did). While doing my aerial gyrations for a second time, and since time was now *standing still,* anyway; I kept my little one-sided conversation going. "Not quite ready for me yet-HUH?" Did I have time for a little chuckle? Hmmm. Then the last "ready or not, here I come, I'm on my way now."

Another excruciating clobber. Again, Hood-Roof-Trunk-Asphalt? Hey it was dark, and time wasn't really on my side, like I thought. Yes I did undulate, (is that dirty?) yet again; only this time my quip came out as "I'm on my wayyyy!" After that came a great big "Wumph."

My entire body lurched up and down and I found myself suddenly, then facing "heads-up." (I win!). When my helmet quit ratcheting my head up and down; I found myself starring up at a beautiful star-light eve. Just one big problem. I had NO ability to move and the most frightening part was, now that I was done with the humorous part of my solo conversation, I really did believe-NO I was sure that I now would be dead soon. Why? Traffic-No. I was just simply and plainly NOT able to breathe! AT All!

Know what happens when you don't breathe? Ya; that's right, you pass-out then die. Laying there surmising my options, I didn't start to reminisce over my now almost duplicate scenario; or how I had wrecked my Kawasaki beauty again. Rather, I was contemplating if I had enough oxygen in my lungs to make it till I receive some help.

Suddenly there was a fella's face bent down right to my nose. I saw him look at me and say "Hey man; they already called the cops, you'll be fine! Just hang in there." Right after that, he was gone.

I'm sorry, but I wasn't counting time. I suddenly felt that someone was trying to take my helmet off, without too much disturbance to moving my head; in case my neck was broke or something. Just suddenly there was a plastic mouth piece over my nose and mouth. All I knew was, that face had a military dress cap on with a shiny black brim. Come to find out, it was one of the police officers, whose voice I instantly recognized from his periodic visits to my motorcycle, ATV, Jet Ski store, which was just one mile down the road.

"Thank God!" I was able to "almost" breathe again. 'What do you mean {almost able" to breathe? I felt the pressure rush of oxygen being shoved down my chest, but I couldn't inhale or exhale on my own.

Still not cognizant of time, I'll say *shortly* after the police got there, and then placed the oxygen on me, I noticed bright lights and red lights flashing, down towards my feet. When I came to the abrupt halt, it was all the way over into the center median, on that big multi-lane boulevard highway. My body was positioned on a forty-five degree angle, to the north bound lanes. Come to think of it, [again] I almost got it again, seeing my head landed only inches from the center traffic light pole. The ambulance came to a stop, just to the East of my feet.

I heard voices and some metal noise, then another body over me, and yet a third person was standing directly over me with the "hugest" set of scissors that I have ever seen. He reached forward and grabbed the bottom of my comfortably beautiful gray leather (color-match) Kawasaki Concours riding jacket. The other EMT held it partially up and this man started cutting right along the side of the zipper, until they got completely cut open. My thoughts "AWE" Not the jacket" they could have just unzipped it.

I heard the stretcher being unfolded, then six arms slid below me, and up and over I was laying on the rolling cot. One of them took my helmet off, and chirped in a grimace like tone "Hi Dave! This *IS* your corner; NO?" Guess what? I didn't respond. They quickly proceeded with pulling the carrier up and then carrying me over to the rescue squad. Once totally in, while the doors were still open, they; the EMT's all started discussing which traumatic hospital they were going to take me to.

The argumentative disagreement seemed to go on and on. Under my oxygen mask, I started blurting, (the best I could) "LOU's! LOU's!" Figuring, quickly, that's where I was kept alive the last time, six years ago. I didn't know if they could even hear me under the mask, and over their arguing. Suddenly one of them said, "Alright; LOU's-Let's get going."

If you forget the rest of this "run-down" (get it rundown?) ha ha. Just go back up to the first chapter and re-read it again; so you know what happened when the "paramedics" dropped me off, at my almost personal medical hotel.

Chapter Nine

The END IS NEAR!

have let it be known, that I'm not much of a gambler. But if *you are,* or know someone who is, just try to figure the *odds* of what I'm about to reiterate.

The <u>Same </u>departure time: 6:00 pm Left the building/business Oak Creek MotorSports Inc.

The <u>Same </u>direction: due NORTH

The <u>Same</u> road/highway US 41/ 27th St. Oak Creek, Wi.

The <u>Same</u> Location: Rawson Ave. crossing US 41

The <u>Same</u> Incident time: 6:02 pm

The <u>Same</u> Vehicle: 1986 Kawasaki Concours (the exact same bike)

The <u>Same</u> Driver: Mr. David Miles

The <u>Same</u> 911 caller: employee at gas station, as 6 years earlier

The <u>Same</u> Police; Three officers from 6 years earlier.

The <u>Same</u> medical facility large traumatic hospital (we'll still call it St. Lou's)

Yes! The same person calling 911 (employee at the Clark gas station).

Eleven! Recount `em. 11 duplicates, replicas, analogous conditions that could hardly be proclaimed as say "man made," or concocted, arranged or manipulated!

The POPE couldn't, the President couldn't, no human's own power. So what shall we call all of these rather encrypted circumstances? {fate-destiny-coincidence-just so happens?}

The extra interesting part of this whole condition, is the fact that when I felt so driven (hah ha) to take a cycle ride for the first time of the year. I ran a cycle shop for three decades, and the desire to ride is stronger than ever.

So I went into the warehouse and being the Vice President, (Oak Creek MotorSports) had my choice of which bike to ride. But I got the "bug" late in the day. As I was walking in back, it dawned on me that I never put any of them on charge. GREAT! Stepping up to each one and turning the ignition, all I got was click, click, and click, or a slow grrr, and then nothing. I never thought to charge any of the batteries that had been sitting dormant now for the fall and winter season. After trying three or four cycles, I came upon my Concours, turning the key, hitting the starter button, it fired right up. (Of course)

So I got on it and pulled it out of the warehouse and locked the overhead door. Then I went around to the front and said "goodnight" to the employees. I locked the door and set the code, then put my; get this, another {duplicate} silver Bell M2 full face helmet on and headed on down the road.

I would love to just enhance and validate this whole incident when I thought it might be best to share again some of the first book. But please simply look toward the front or read my first book "The DOA Who Made It". Now I am about to emulate my

July first 27ᵗʰ & Rawson activity, for yet another reason, which I sincerely hope you will agree with.

So here we go AGAIN!

The only thing to fear... is *HELL* itself!

We give strong accolades to men and women of the past, such as Magellan, Columbus, Lief Erickson, or say John Glen; in other words (great explorers) of the *unknown*.) And I believe we should do that rightfully so.

Say even someone like Steve Jobs, or any of the courageous people that sacrifice "all" to start up a new venture. Because they challenged the mysteries of the *unrevealed*. But taking the chance that what they/you believe, gives you the fortitude to go further.

Is it chance, luck, good fortune, "ballsy"? Whether you like it or not...it always takes *FAITH*. In other words, "It" is what you believe to *be* either true or possible. Well, guess what? That is a lot of what it takes to prepare for the ultimate eternal unknown-DEATH!

Have all of the great adventurers just gone out on a hunch? With absolutely NO input from either their education known to them at the time, or maybe reports of what others have already discovered?

Oh how we all like to look back (after having learned that the old discoveries were either wrong, or only partially correct) and say to ourselves or others "see they sure didn't get it right, so how can I believe anything today?

157

Example, for millennia, people believed that the sun revolved around the earth, and that the earth was flat. WRONG! But that didn't eliminate the sun or the earth. It didn't change anybody's life in the 14th, or 15th, century. The point is just because things don't all take place the way we think they do, doesn't dissolve the realities

So far, I haven't used the word {*trust*} much yet, but those two words (faith & trust) do correlate quite close, as I am sure that you would be willing to agree. Look... we all know that it takes faith to trust and trust to have faith, in either someone/something/somewhere. NO?

If you don't trust you don't have faith; say maybe in your ideas, or accomplishments or even in someone else's words or deeds either. Funny, isn't it that all of our U.S. money hard and soft all say *"IN GOD WE Trust"* Trusting a boss, a spouse, a friend all take faith. Then when that trust is broken, it takes almost forever to regain that trust. Then it usually takes "forgiveness" from one or both parties. And I'm sure you'll agree, that is usually very hard to accomplish.

One big problem with trust is that when we have faith or trust in someone or something we must realize that if we explode our faith/trust, over and above what should be there, we automatically default to the premise that *NONE* "of it/them" can be trusted At ALL!.

Tell me, that you don't know somebody (maybe yourself) that "counted on god to heal or protect their loved one; only to turn on God when he didn't meet their expectations.

Were they God's fault? Only someone who supposedly believed in God, to begin with could say "YES! It's all His fault"

So know I can justify myself in "not believing in Him anymore. {convenient...NO?}

As I shared in my last book; having been killed by that dead drunk, the sweet little black gal, who was the chaplain on my floor, told me the whole story and ended our conversation with "Now you know what must be done! You have to forgive the man that just killed you, whether he asks for forgiveness or not." Okay so maybe I could forgive him, but trust him too? I don't think so. Remember "Once burned Twice shy?"

So does that make my forgiveness unreal or just phony? Probably, because true forgiveness is to "forget." That is God's kind of forgiveness. When He forgive your sins he treats you like you have never or will never sin. (That's TRUE Forgiveness). Do you really believe that God could/would forgive you; even while knowing that your so-called repentance is either very short lived or just plain phony?

"Com-on" you say. In the Greek and Hebrew definitions of that concept, it does mean to *forget*. The word "justification or to justify in the biblical places, is that the person is IN Total innocence to that regard. Merriam Webster's dictionary for justify, in the religious meaning is "To declare innocent or guiltless... absolve, acquit."

God wants every-one of us to be "justified" so we can spend eternity in Glory with Him! Not in utter darkness and depravity of damnation, due to our sin, and disbelief.

Having now passed through both side of *death's* door; my earnest desire is for all readers of this book or of "The DOA Who made It," to certainly take to heart, just exactly what it is that I am ultimately trying to convince each one of you, of. The validity of life is proof enough, just by your reading these words. I want to say desperately that the proof of death (that I am now sure everyone will agree to as well) is just as real.

The proof of "eternal existence is just as real. Although there is one great big "caveat." Many of you simply either don't, or are maybe rather skeptically" unsure of the reality of a heaven or hell. Really?...Is this all there is? Seriously, You can believe tht?

Life after Death...?

I truly empathize with both of those suspicions. My full "two stories," have been penned to relieve the doubt or distrust of the authenticity of those entities.

Sure there is a cacophony of religious sounds "out there;" all proclaiming to have the correct answer. But ask yourself "What other spiritual (we'll call it force) proclaims to have a "Savior?" Where else can you find, over three thousand individuals see for themselves the proof of the resurrection? (Holy Bible, Acts 1:9) Why can a criminal judge take the (exact matching, or at least close) testimony of just two; to make an acquittal or conviction, yet we can't believe the testimony of 3000 or written testimony of so many, that Jesus Did DIE and then escape the clutches of either temporary or eternal obliteration. They saw him rise up into the clouds on what is known in the Jewish and Christian time called Pentecost!

A legal court of law needs TWO, yes just TWO witnesses to verify the proof of something. A mass of men and women proclaiming the resurrection of the innocent person raising up into the clouds. With such outlandish and antipathetic blatant proclamations made in the first century; why wasn't there some sort of refute, even back then, either by the Jewish hierarchy or the Roman's and their legal system?

How can we ever believe *anything* that comes on the screen of the phone, tablet, or laptop, or off of the internet? But not be able to accept that our many imperfections in life; which the Bible calls *SIN,* aren't a valid *disgust,* to a pure holy righteous God? But oh, how we just love to use HIM as our "scapegoat" for all the wrongs we experience.

If you can't or don't believe in *Him,* "God?" Why do so many people; maybe like yourself...proclaim to have the authority to put a curse on someone or something else, while calling on His name? "OH My God; God No, GOD damn, or even say 'for God's sake," Hmmm, Or sometimes even "God Bless it." We all have to agree that it is the name of authority; NO ?

Are YOU or Me or Us (people) just too-proud to submit ourselves to some or any form of creator that expects perfection? The knowing of, that otherwise there will be consequences for our disobedience? Yes I have been right there too. Recognized by God as a sinner.

There is no questioning the clarity of exasperating horror. Being the case; how can somebody say "I don't care if there is a Hell or not, I'll be with my buddies, havin' a good time (in Milwaukee it's always 'having a beer) anyway." *Eternal Torment* isn't something that a person has actually ever experienced; and most of us would rather not even accept the likely-hood of.

You'll say, "How can such a {loving} God, do that to people after all they have to suffer through right here on earth, already?" The answer is short, but not sweet.

News and history channels, and numerous documentaries show huge gory gross, despicable torment's, that man can and does do to fellow man, either over greed, control, power, or just anger bringing fights and war etc. So why is it so hard to envision "deserved" torment for all of the "wrongs" done to a holy righteous, sovereign god (creator, founder, & sustainer) of the entire universe?

Really; what does it take, (besides submission) to accept an "all empowered" (entity that could easily create a _mature_ universe, solar system, planet and everything else;) that "just so happens to be just the right distance from the Sun, tilted at just the right number of degrees, with just the right atmosphere to sustain life with just the right amount of water, with just the right chemicals to allow life to persist?

Eight Billion yeas of SEX! ???

I have never used this paradigm, while trying to convey the validity of a "creator" in this universe of existence; but since I am a licensed school teacher, I go to six different school districts, here is Southeastern Wisconsin, to be a substitute for mostly high school and middle school classes.

Recently, I was called by a school district near to the south side of Milwaukee. They expressed their desperate need of a "sub" in about an hour. So when a teacher takes an assignment, they send a confirmation through emails.

They confirmed the school, and location, then the class/teacher/room/ and time. What made this request so interesting, was, that there was no room listed or class type; say English, Biology, Algebra, etc.

When I arrived, they gave me my lanyard, with the tag proclaiming my substitute position, but NO folder with lesson plans, class times, and school rules. But the administrator woman, just handed me the lanyard. Soo..I quickly asked "which classroom, and what the absent teacher's class is about? Don't I need a key to get in the room?" "Not this one." Came right back at me.

Very, shall we say hesitantly, and evasive, the nervous receptionist finally said in a stuttering voice, that it was "Mr. so & so. And his room is just behind this office, around the corner." "Alright then" I acknowledged, then I queried…"What kind of class is it, science, math, English?" "Ah...Ah… No Mr. so & so, takes care of the "at risk" juniors and seniors." While saying that, I could have sworn, that she was aiming for the door, to block my retreat- out of the room and building!

I (now almost fearing for my life, said) "Oh; you mean, the special needs kids?" "NO.no" Came right back at me. These are the boys, who don't want to be here, and they will usually let you *know that* {right away}! Here is the telephone number of the office, if you need it.

I followed the custodian, who unlocked the door, and I entered the voided room. As each class bell rang, I would get one or two big strong healthy looking young men. They pretty much just ignored my presence, unless I asked them their name, for the attendance sheet. I would get a grunt, or growl. And that was about it.

After lunch period and nearer the end of the day, I thought "hey this isn't so bad." Then fourth hour bell rang and slowly the room filled up. "Oh-boy, here we go." I thought to myself. I suddenly was confronted with eleven high-school juniors, not one of them had any interest in being in that room; especially with a bulky smaller old man, like me, around.

"What are my options?" I thought to myself. They started to walk around the room, and wouldn't even acknowledge my request of names for attendance. A few were in the back center of the room talking, about what; I had no idea. Maybe to my demise. "All guts-few brains," I veered over towards them, with a look, like "stay away man- if you don't want to be around here or you'll get hurt...look."

Of course the only topic they conversed was SEX! That was it, and not spoken of in a nice medicinal sort of way, either. I believe their conversation was solely designed to see who could intimidate me. Somehow, one of them commented on what they would be doing if they were ever get to go to say France on one of the "nude beaches." I piped up and said that I had been there, and many other places with nude beaches.

Guess What! They suddenly all turned to me and looked with surprise and started asking me a lot of questions, about my experiences. There were smiles coming on their faces, while I "curtly" described some of my many trips to places like Tahiti, Rio De Janeiro, Caen France, and other exotic destinations.

You would have thought that I was the "coolest-dude" that they ever met. All of their questions were focused on one consideration; and that was it.

One fella, kept say "Oh my God." I looked at him and asked "Are you planning on becoming a priest, or pastor, or maybe a Rabbi, or e-mom?" The whole room broke out into a roar of laughter. I continued, with a smile on my face by saying that "hey your always talking about God, I thought maybe that was your interest.

"NO Man" I don't believe in no god." "Really?" I asked. "I'm an Atheist; I think." Came back.

"Oooh"…I quipped. "So you're an evolutionist then too; Nooo?" "Well sort-ta" he stammered back. "Alright!" I said. "Let's say that there is NO God of any sort." They knew that I was heading somewhere with this, and it got quieter, as they all turned to listen, to me say something about God in a public school.

"Let's say that you are right…that there is NO GOD; just evolution, OKAY" Many head nods agreed. "Do you believe that this {whole thing-universe} I motioned all around? Do you guys' believe that in {only eight-8 yes eight billion years}, that, say an ameba, that washed up on shore somewhere, could have grown that male appendage, you are all so proud of, and persst in telling me all about, and put it in the right place, not say in your arm-pit, or your right hip." And all of that turned out juusst right, so it was the right size too?"

"I'll tell ya guys, I'm more <u>willin'</u> to bet that God did that for ya." They all turned to me and sheepishly and rather startlingly meek, nodded up and down, and said; almost in a chanting chorus. "Ya that makes more sense, now."

I looked heaven ward, and smiled when the bell suddenly rang. They <u>All</u> said (a form of good bye) to me, as they departed, leaving me safe and peaceful.

Who or whatever you are… just give that concept a thought for a moment. Can anybody who still calls themselves a scientist, really, honestly, truly believe that "say something like evolution could make a perfect working stomach, or kidney, say a pancreas? Much less a brain, or a perfect working organ like a heart that beats an average of 2.5 billion times.

Just so a person doesn't have to take responsibility for their faults (sins), they'll concoct a concept like evolution just so they don't have to answer for their misdeeds. How scary sad.

There are so many valid proofs of a "New Creation" of this earth and this universe, but it seems everyone wants to believe these scientific "pundits." You can't really call them scientists when they "speculate, believe, "many now agree." I was taught to understand that scientist gather FACTS! No they don't just use their so called educated guesses. To make true scientific conclusive type insinuated facts.

But guess what? They have to *believe* their carbon 14 type compilations, even when it has proven wrong and ineffective repeatedly. Even the "Scopes Trial" did that!

My point behind all of this is to alert you to the fact that "it all takes FAITH!" But now I have gone beyond that step. I was *never* intending to "discover" these truths over and above anyone else. But for some unknown reason, (to me) I was chosen to be made aware of these proofs, and miracles.

My heart's desire for this book and the DOA Who Made It! Is to inform YOU of these events and conditions, to hopefully cause you to amend you beliefs; to accept GOD and His son Jesus Christ, as your own personal Savior.

Another way of being "politically correct" these days, (especially as a teacher) is to not say that the "Bible says", but rather, as I tell the kids at different times "an ancient document says — —." Then all is {well}. My example is when I was teaching an

8th grade class in Oak Creek, Wisconsin; we were to watch a You-tube video on the real-life stories of a woman who as a little girl suffered in one of Adolph Hitler's "death camps" like Dachas.

The students were almost mesmerized by what they were watching. When it was over, and just before the class ended and they were to leave. A couple of them said things like "how could any human do things like that? Especially to other people? I said to the kids that there is an "ancient document" that says "the heart is deceitful and exceedingly wicked."

They all were deeply moved and listened intently to those words. I NEVER said anything about {The Bible}. Hmmm. Now it is accepted

For the last six or seven years now; my wife and I have been attending a really excellent church, on the southwest side of Milwaukee in a suburb called Greenfield, Wisconsin.

What we enjoy and appreciate about this church "Layton Avenue Baptist Church" is that it is very focused on doing what they/we believe God is having Hisbelievers' in Him to do, while on this planet.

After several years of being prodded to sell our properties on a busy highway and corner in that city of Greenfield, Wisconsin. Things started to get real serious about a huge business development that was being arranged in a huge "block" of property ad ours was included n that scheme of plans.

Finally, after arriving at a "suitable" price we sold our properties and bought some land about six blocks farther to the west or our existing rounds. All s "well and good" with all of this money now in our account, but with the purchase and cost of the land then the building, we were going to still fall way short

167

of the need funds to put up a new building and make all of the need changes to the grounds as well.

Then the "neatest" thing happened rather quietly. The church leadership filled out a twenty three page application with an organization that has been doing "this" for many years now. "This?" Yes! This non-profit organization known as "Builders for Christ" after reading our answers on the long-long application discuss-pray and decide just which and where that they will work with. They chose our church this year.

Ok...okay- do what? You ask. They will come from all over the country and on their own time, travel, living and easting costs, with their own tools; and they will build our church for us after we have the foundation and floor in place. ABSOLUTELY FREE! Can you believe that?

Yes! They all voluntarily come for the whole summer in one or two week increments and erect and finish off our church at no-cost except the needed lumber.

And we are NOT Even Amish!

Call it "happen-stance, good-luck, just lucky or simply "good for us" but can you picture some "evolutionists or atheists" doing something like that for others who you don't even know? That is simply seen by all of us as GOD at Work!

As I close this book, I have something for you to ponder. My hope and prayer was that you liked the book (s) and really got something out of it (them) and that you might see the need and possible urgency of the fact that it takes a personal commitment to reach-out to God and ask to receive Jesus Christ, God's own son to be your savior.

Interesting "tid bit" to mull over. Jesus Christ of history is never or no-where called

The _Late_ Jesus Christ!
Because…
He IS ALIVE! And I have talked directly with Him.
Please believe in HIM for your eternal salvation!

Please don't just say "HELL NO!"
Thanks Dave

CPSIA information can be obtained
at www.ICGtesting.com
Printed in the USA
LVOW06s2047220616
493549LV00005BA/14/P